FLAVORS
FROM FLORIDA

# Fit, Fresh & Fast

Fit, Fresh & Fast—that's
Florida Citrus, now pre-
sented in ways you've
never seen before! You'll
discover new ways to use citrus
as an ingredient to replace
high-fat foods and sugar while
enhancing flavor. We've taken
the fresh taste of citrus and
blended it into recipes that are
bursting with flavor, easy to
make, and filled with the
healthful nutrients of nature's
sunniest fruits. To help you
enjoy the fruits of your labor,
we've streamlined the recipes
for easy preparation. We're
proud to offer these innovative
ideas from the Sunshine State
and the Florida Citrus Growers.
Any way you fix it, citrus from
Florida is Fit, Fresh & Fast.

Pictured on the cover:
Caribbean-Grilled Chicken with Citrus (see recipe, page 4)

# Fit, Fresh & Fast

## FLAVORS FROM FLORIDA

## CONTENTS

This seal assures you that every recipe in **Fit, Fresh & Fast** has been tested in the *Better Homes and Gardens*® Test Kitchen. This means that each recipe is practical and reliable, and meets high standards of taste appeal.
© Copyright 1995 Florida Department of Citrus.
© Copyright 1995 Meredith Corporation. All rights reserved.
Printed in the U.S.A. Produced by Meredith Publishing Services, 1912 Grand Ave., Des Moines, IA 50309-3379.

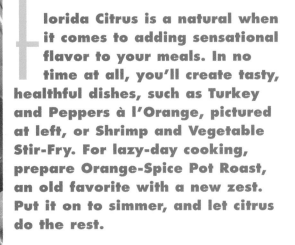

# Easy Entrées

**F**lorida Citrus is a natural when it comes to adding sensational flavor to your meals. In no time at all, you'll create tasty, healthful dishes, such as Turkey and Peppers à l'Orange, pictured at left, or Shrimp and Vegetable Stir-Fry. For lazy-day cooking, prepare Orange-Spice Pot Roast, an old favorite with a new zest. Put it on to simmer, and let citrus do the rest.

← Turkey and Peppers à l'Orange
(see recipe, page 5)

3

# Caribbean-Grilled Chicken with Citrus

*The spicy orange marinade gives grilled chicken an irresistible tangy flavor. Pictured on the cover.*

| | |
|---|---|
| 1 | 14½-ounce can chicken broth |
| ¾ | cup frozen Florida Orange Juice Concentrate, thawed |
| 2 | tablespoons red wine vinegar |
| 1 | tablespoon Jamaican jerk seasoning |
| 2 | teaspoons finely shredded Florida Orange Peel |
| 2 | cloves garlic, minced |
| 6 | skinless, boneless medium chicken breast halves |
| 4 | teaspoons cornstarch |
| 3 | cups hot cooked rice |
| 2 | Florida Red Grapefruit, peeled, sliced, and seeded |
| 2 | Florida Oranges, peeled, sliced, and seeded |
| ¼ | cup sliced green onions |
| | Green onion brushes* (optional) |

In a nonmetallic bowl stir together broth, thawed orange juice concentrate, vinegar, jerk seasoning, orange peel, and garlic. Cover and chill *half* of the mixture for sauce.

Rinse chicken; pat dry. In a plastic bag set in a shallow dish combine chicken and remaining orange mixture. Close bag and chill for 2 to 24 hours, turning bag occasionally to distribute marinade.

Drain off marinade and reserve. Place chicken on grill rack of an uncovered grill. Brush with some of the reserved marinade. Grill directly over *medium* coals 12 to 15 minutes or until chicken is tender and no longer pink, turning once. Discard marinade.

Meanwhile, for sauce, in a medium saucepan combine the remaining chilled orange mixture with cornstarch. Cook and stir over medium heat until thickened and bubbly. Cook and stir for 2 minutes more.

To serve, spoon rice on each of 6 dinner plates. Arrange grapefruit and orange slices on each plate; place 1 piece of chicken on top of grapefruit and orange slices. Spoon fruit sauce over chicken and fruit. Sprinkle with green onions. If desired, garnish with green onion brushes. Serves 6.

*Note: To make green onion brush garnish, slice roots from end of a green onion and remove most of the green portion. Make slashes at both ends of the onion piece for fringes. Place in ice water to curl the ends.

*Per serving (with rice):* 329 cal., 24 g pro., 49 g carbo., 4 g total fat (1 g sat. fat), 54 mg cholesterol, 3 g dietary fiber, 304 mg sodium. Daily Value: 83% vit. C, 27% folate, 33% thiamine, 12% riboflavin, 76% niacin, 15% iron, 26% potassium.

## Nutrition Note

At the end of each recipe in this book, important nutrition information is provided. This is how we analyze the recipes:

• When a choice of ingredients is given, we use the first ingredient in the analysis.

• We use the first serving size listed when a range is given.

• Optional ingredients are not included in the calculations.

• Numbers are rounded off to the nearest whole number.

• Vitamin C amounts may vary due to heat applied during cooking.

• We've listed the Daily Values for selected vitamins and minerals whenever the recipe provides 10 percent or more of the recommended amount.

# Turkey and Peppers à l'Orange

*Easy enough for every day, yet impressive enough for guests, this dish offers a succulent orange-basil sauce. Pictured on pages 2–3.*

| | |
|---|---|
| ¾ | cup frozen Florida Orange Juice *Concentrate*, thawed |
| ⅔ | cup reduced-sodium chicken broth or water |
| 2 | tablespoons snipped fresh basil or 2 teaspoons dried basil, crushed |
| 2 | teaspoons cornstarch |
| 2 | teaspoons snipped fresh tarragon or ½ teaspoon dried tarragon, crushed |
| ¼ | teaspoon salt |
| ⅛ | teaspoon black pepper Nonstick spray coating |
| 1 | pound turkey breast slices or tenderloins, cut ¼ inch thick |
| 1 | teaspoon olive oil or cooking oil |
| 1½ | cups thinly sliced red or green sweet pepper |
| 1 | medium onion, sliced and separated into rings |
| 4 | Florida Oranges, peeled, sliced, and seeded Fresh basil sprigs Hot cooked rice (optional) |

For sauce, in a small bowl stir together thawed orange juice concentrate, broth, snipped basil, cornstarch, tarragon, salt, and black pepper. Set aside.

Spray an unheated 12-inch skillet with nonstick coating. Rinse turkey; pat dry. Heat skillet over medium heat. Add turkey slices and cook 3 to 5 minutes on each side or until no longer pink. Remove turkey slices to a platter; cover and keep warm.

Add oil to the skillet, if necessary. Add sweet pepper and onion slices to skillet; cook about 4 minutes or until vegetables are tender, stirring occasionally. Stir sauce; add to skillet. Cook and stir until thickened and bubbly. Cook and stir for 2 minutes more.

To serve, arrange turkey and orange slices on a serving platter. Spoon vegetables onto platter and spoon sauce over all. Garnish with basil sprigs. If desired, serve with hot cooked rice. Makes 4 servings.

**Per serving (without rice):** *266 cal., 23 g pro., 40 g carbo., 3 g total fat (0 g sat. fat), 55 mg cholesterol, 5 g dietary fiber, 331 mg sodium. Daily Value: 222% vit. C, 33% vit. A, 61% folate, 33% thiamine, 16% riboflavin, 47% niacin, 12% calcium, 11% iron, 44% potassium.*

To peel a citrus fruit, first thoroughly wash it with tap water. (Don't wash any fruit or vegetable with detergent.) Cut a thin slice off each end of the fruit. Set it on one end and cut a strip of peel from the top to the bottom, removing as much white membrane as possible. Continue removing strips around the fruit.

# Florida-Style Barbecued Chicken

*Grapefruit juice concentrate adds a distinctive zip to the barbecue sauce. The hearty sauce also works wonders with beef or pork ribs.*

| | |
|---|---|
| ½ | cup chopped onion |
| ¾ | cup water |
| 1 | cup catsup |
| ⅓ | cup frozen Florida Grapefruit Juice Concentrate, thawed |
| 1 | to 2 tablespoons brown sugar |
| 1 | tablespoon Worcestershire sauce |
| 1 | tablespoon prepared mustard |
| 3 | pounds meaty chicken pieces (breasts, thighs, and drumsticks) |
| | Red and White Florida Grapefruit Points (see directions, page 78) |

For barbecue sauce, in a medium saucepan cook onion in *2 tablespoons* of the water about 5 minutes or until onion is tender. Stir in remaining water, catsup, thawed grapefruit juice concentrate, brown sugar, Worcestershire sauce, and mustard. Bring just to boiling; reduce heat. Cover and simmer for 30 minutes.

Remove skin from chicken pieces. Rinse chicken; pat dry. Place chicken, bone side up, on the grill rack of an uncovered grill. Grill directly over *medium* coals for 20 minutes. Turn chicken; grill for 15 to 25 minutes more or until chicken is tender and no longer pink. Brush the chicken occasionally with some of the barbecue sauce during the last 10 minutes of grilling.

Heat remaining barbecue sauce and pass with chicken. Garnish with grapefruit points. Store any remaining barbecue sauce in a covered container in the refrigerator for up to 1 week. Makes 6 servings.

**Per serving:** *312 cal., 37 g pro., 19 g carbo., 9 g total fat (3 g sat. fat), 109 mg cholesterol, 1 g dietary fiber, 651 mg sodium. Daily Value: 27% vit. C, 10% folate, 15% thiamine, 22% riboflavin, 89% niacin, 13% iron, 30% potassium.*

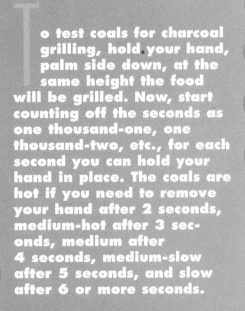

To test coals for charcoal grilling, hold your hand, palm side down, at the same height the food will be grilled. Now, start counting off the seconds as one thousand-one, one thousand-two, etc., for each second you can hold your hand in place. The coals are hot if you need to remove your hand after 2 seconds, medium-hot after 3 seconds, medium after 4 seconds, medium-slow after 5 seconds, and slow after 6 or more seconds.

## Orange-Glazed Chicken

*Spicy orange glaze makes this grill-or-broil chicken dish a year-round favorite.*

| | |
|---|---|
| ¾ | cup frozen Florida Orange Juice **Concentrate**, thawed |
| ⅓ | cup honey |
| ¼ | cup light soy sauce |
| 1½ | teaspoons five-spice powder |
| ¾ | teaspoon garlic powder |
| 3 | pounds meaty chicken pieces (breasts, thighs, and drumsticks) |
| 2 | Florida Oranges, thinly sliced |

For glaze, in a small mixing bowl combine thawed orange juice concentrate, honey, soy sauce, five-spice powder, and garlic powder. Set the mixture aside.

Remove skin from chicken pieces. Rinse chicken; pat dry. In a covered grill arrange *medium-hot* coals around a drip pan. Test for *medium* heat above the pan. Place chicken, bone side down, on the grill rack over the drip pan. Cover and grill for 50 to 60 minutes or until chicken is tender and no longer pink, brushing occasionally with glaze during the last 10 minutes of grilling.

Heat any remaining glaze; pass with chicken. Garnish with orange slices. Makes 6 servings.

**To broil:** Place chicken, bone side up, on the unheated rack of a broiler pan. Broil 4 to 5 inches from the heat about 20 minutes or until lightly browned. Turn chicken, bone side down, and broil for 5 to 15 minutes more or until chicken is tender and no longer pink. Brush occasionally with glaze during last 5 minutes of cooking. Serve as directed above.

**To cook by direct-grill method:** Place chicken, bone side up, on the grill rack of an uncovered grill. Grill directly over *medium* coals for 20 minutes. Turn chicken; grill for 15 to 25 minutes more or until chicken is tender and no longer pink, brushing occasionally with glaze during the last 10 minutes of grilling. Serve as directed at left.

**Per serving:** *362 cal., 37 g pro., 32 g carbo., 9 g total fat (3 g sat. fat), 109 mg cholesterol, 1 g dietary fiber, 447 mg sodium. Daily Value: 64% vit. C, 34% folate, 21% thiamine, 23% riboflavin, 90% niacin, 14% iron, 30% potassium.*

## Chicken with Citrus-Leek Sauce

| | |
|---|---|
| 4 | skinless, boneless medium chicken breast halves (12 ounces total) |
| 1 | medium leek, thinly sliced |
| 2 | teaspoons olive or cooking oil |
| ⅓ | cup frozen Florida Orange Juice **Concentrate**, thawed |
| ⅓ | cup water |
| 3 | tablespoons dry white wine or chicken broth |
| 2 | tablespoons orange marmalade |
| 2 | cups hot cooked couscous or rice (optional) |

Rinse chicken; pat dry. Set aside. In a large skillet cook leek in hot oil over medium heat for 2 minutes; remove from skillet and set aside. If necessary, add additional oil to skillet. Add chicken to skillet; cook for 8 to 10 minutes or until tender and no longer pink, turning once. Remove chicken from skillet; cover and keep warm.

Add thawed orange juice concentrate, water, wine or broth, and marmalade to the skillet. Bring to boiling; reduce heat. Boil gently, uncovered, about 8 minutes or until mixture cooks down to about ¼ cup. Return chicken and leeks to skillet, turning chicken to glaze with sauce. Heat through. Serve with couscous or rice, if desired. Serves 4.

**Per serving (without couscous):** *203 cal., 20 g pro., 17 g carbo., 5 g total fat (1g sat. fat), 54 mg cholesterol, 1 g dietary fiber, 57 mg sodium. Daily Value: 35% vit. C, 25% folate, 11% thiamine, 61% niacin, 17% potassium.*

# Orange-Ginger Chicken Stir-Fry

| | |
|---|---|
| 1½ | pounds skinless, boneless chicken breast halves |
| ¾ | cup frozen Florida Orange Juice *Concentrate*, thawed |
| ¾ | cup water |
| 2 | tablespoons cornstarch |
| 2 | tablespoons dry sherry (optional) |
| 2 | teaspoons instant chicken bouillon granules |
| ⅛ | teaspoon salt |
| ⅛ | teaspoon ground red pepper |
| 2 | tablespoons olive oil or cooking oil |
| 2 | to 3 teaspoons grated fresh gingerroot or ½ teaspoon ground ginger |
| 3 | cloves garlic, minced |
| 2 | medium carrots, thinly bias sliced |
| 2 | medium zucchini, cut into thin, 2-inch strips |
| 1 | medium yellow summer squash, cut into thin, 2-inch strips |
| 1 | 8-ounce can sliced water chestnuts, drained Orange Rice (optional) (see recipe, page 41) Green onions (optional) |

Rinse chicken; pat dry. Cut chicken into bite-size strips; set aside. Reserve *1 tablespoon* of the thawed orange juice concentrate for Orange Rice. For sauce, in a small bowl stir together remaining orange juice concentrate, water, cornstarch, sherry (if desired), bouillon granules, salt, and red pepper; set aside.

Pour oil into a wok or 12-inch skillet. (Add more oil, if necessary, during cooking.) Preheat over medium-high heat.

Stir-fry gingerroot (if using ground ginger, add with sauce ingredients) and garlic for 15 seconds. Add carrots; stir-fry for 2 minutes. Add zucchini and yellow summer squash; stir-fry for 2 minutes more. Remove vegetables from the wok or skillet.

Add *half* of the chicken to the wok. Stir-fry for 2 to 3 minutes or until no pink remains. Remove chicken. Repeat with remaining chicken. Return all chicken to wok. Push chicken from the center. Stir sauce; pour into center of wok. Cook and stir until thickened and bubbly. Return vegetables to wok; add water chestnuts. Cook and stir 2 minutes more or until heated through. Serve immediately with Orange Rice. Garnish with green onions, if desired. Makes 6 to 8 servings.

**Per serving (without rice):** *292 cal., 29 g pro., 25 g carbo., 9 g total fat (2 g sat. fat), 72 mg cholesterol, 3 g dietary fiber, 424 mg sodium. Daily Value: 93% vit. C, 90% vit. A, 43% folate, 23% thiamine, 14% riboflavin, 86% niacin, 12% iron, 37% potassium.*

# Grilled Honey-Soy Chicken Sandwiches

*For a quick, easy meal, marinate the chicken the night before. The next day, you'll only need 12 minutes to cook the chicken. Here's another time-saver: Toast the buns on the grill or under the broiler while the chicken cooks.*

| | |
|---|---|
| 1/3 | cup frozen Florida Orange Juice Concentrate, thawed |
| 2 | tablespoons light soy sauce |
| 2 | tablespoons honey |
| 1 | teaspoon lemon-pepper seasoning |
| 1 | teaspoon ground ginger |
| 1/4 | teaspoon garlic powder |
| 4 | skinless, boneless medium chicken breast halves (12 ounces total) |
| 4 | whole wheat hamburger buns Lettuce leaves |
| 2 | or 3 plum tomatoes, thinly sliced |

For marinade, in a shallow nonmetallic dish combine thawed orange juice concentrate, soy sauce, honey, lemon-pepper seasoning, ginger, and garlic powder. Set aside.

Rinse chicken; pat dry. Place each breast half between 2 pieces of plastic wrap. Working from center to the edges, pound chicken lightly with the flat side of a meat mallet to an even thickness. Remove plastic wrap. Place chicken pieces in marinade. Cover and chill 4 to 6 hours or overnight, turning chicken occasionally.

Remove chicken from marinade, reserving marinade. To grill, place chicken on the grill rack of an uncovered grill. Grill directly over *medium* coals about 12 minutes or until chicken is tender and no longer pink, turning and brushing chicken with marinade once, halfway through cooking. Discard the marinade.

To serve, split buns and place on grill rack or broiler pan for 1 to 2 minutes to toast. Serve chicken breasts on toasted buns. Top each with lettuce leaves and tomato slices. Makes 4 servings.

**To broil:** Place chicken on the unheated rack of a broiler pan. Broil 4 to 5 inches from heat for 7 to 8 minutes or until chicken is tender and no longer pink, turning and brushing chicken with marinade once, halfway through cooking. Discard marinade. Serve as above.

**Per serving:** *277 cal., 25 g pro., 32 g carbo., 6 g total fat (1 g sat. fat), 54 mg cholesterol, 3 g dietary fiber, 488 mg sodium. Daily Value: 25% vit. C, 28% folate, 31% thiamine, 21% riboflavin, 78% niacin, 19% iron, 21% potassium.*

# Broiled Swordfish with Tangerine Relish

*Sweet tangerines and snappy jalapeño peppers make a masterful combo to serve with any fish. If you prefer a milder relish, use only half of the pepper.*

| | |
|---|---|
| 1 | pound fresh or frozen swordfish or halibut steaks (about ¾ inch thick) |
| ½ | cup Florida Tangerine or Orange Juice |
| 2 | tablespoons brown sugar |
| 2 | tablespoons red wine vinegar |
| | Nonstick spray coating |
| 2 | Florida Tangerines, peeled, seeded, and chopped |
| 1 | medium red onion, chopped |
| 2 | tablespoons snipped parsley |
| 1 | small jalapeño pepper, seeded and finely chopped |
| 1 | large clove garlic, minced |
| | Parsley sprigs (optional) |

Thaw fish, if frozen. Cut into 4 serving-size portions. In a small skillet combine tangerine or orange juice, brown sugar, and vinegar. Bring mixture just to boiling; reduce heat. Simmer, uncovered, for 5 to 6 minutes or until mixture becomes syrupy, stirring often. Remove from heat.

Spray the unheated rack of a broiler pan with nonstick coating. Place swordfish or halibut on rack. Brush both sides of fish with *1 tablespoon* of the juice mixture. Broil 4 inches from the heat 6 to 8 minutes or until fish begins to flake easily with a fork.

Meanwhile, for relish, in a medium bowl combine chopped tangerines, red onion, snipped parsley, jalapeño pepper, and garlic. Add remaining juice mixture. Toss gently to mix. Serve fish with relish. Garnish with parsley sprigs, if desired. Makes 4 servings.

**Per serving:** *193 cal., 22 g pro., 15 g carbo., 5 g total fat (1 g sat. fat), 43 mg cholesterol, 1 g dietary fiber, 136 mg sodium. Daily Value: 31% vit. C, 12% vit. A, 11% folate, 11% thiamine, 10% riboflavin, 76% niacin, 25% potassium.*

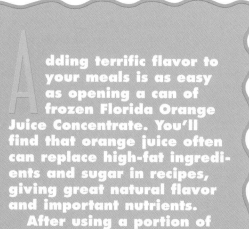

Adding terrific flavor to your meals is as easy as opening a can of frozen Florida Orange Juice Concentrate. You'll find that orange juice often can replace high-fat ingredients and sugar in recipes, giving great natural flavor and important nutrients.

After using a portion of a can, mix the remaining concentrate with water according to the chart on page 59 for ready-to-serve orange juice.

# Poached Fillets and Vegetables with Orange Sauce

1   pound fresh or frozen skinless orange roughy or cod fillets (about ½ inch thick)
2   carrots, cut into thin, bite-size strips
⅔   cup water
½   cup sliced celery
⅓   cup frozen Florida Orange Juice Concentrate, thawed
1   teaspoon snipped fresh basil or ¼ teaspoon dried basil, crushed
½   teaspoon instant chicken bouillon granules
2   teaspoons cornstarch
2   tablespoons cold water

Thaw fish, if frozen. Cut into 4 serving-size portions. In a large skillet combine carrots, the ⅔ cup water, the celery, thawed orange juice concentrate, basil, and chicken bouillon granules. Bring mixture just to boiling. Carefully add fish. Return just to boiling; reduce heat. Cover and simmer for 4 to 6 minutes or until fish begins to flake easily with a fork. Transfer fish, carrots, and celery to a serving platter. Cover and keep warm.

For sauce, strain the cooking liquid, if desired. Return the liquid to skillet. Stir together cornstarch and the 2 tablespoons cold water. Stir into liquid in skillet. Cook and stir until thickened and bubbly. Cook and stir 2 minutes more. To serve, spoon the sauce over fish. Makes 4 servings.

**Per serving:** *137 cal., 17 g pro., 15 g carbo., 1 g total fat (0 g sat. fat), 22 mg cholesterol, 2 g dietary fiber, 208 mg sodium. Daily Value: 41% vit. C, 130% vit. A, 29% folate, 20% thiamine, 16% riboflavin, 27% niacin, 32% potassium.*

# Grilled Orange-Marinated Fish

*Add some Florida style to this meal with grilled sweet peppers, zucchini, and yellow summer squash. Simply cut vegetables into quarters lengthwise, brush with olive oil, and place on the grill rack while the fish cooks. Allow 8 to 10 minutes for peppers and 5 to 6 minutes for squash, turning occasionally.*

1   to 1½ pounds fresh or frozen grouper steaks or red snapper fillets (about 1 inch thick)
¾   cup Citrus Base (see recipe, page 43) Florida Orange Slices

Thaw fish, if frozen. Place fish in a plastic bag set in a shallow dish; add Citrus Base. Close bag. Marinate fish in the refrigerator for 2 to 4 hours, turning bag occasionally.

Remove fish from bag. Discard marinade. Place steaks on the greased grill rack of an uncovered grill or place fillets in a well-greased grill basket. Grill directly over *medium* coals until fish begins to flake easily with a fork, turning once (allow 4 to 6 minutes per ½-inch thickness). Garnish with orange slices. Makes 4 to 6 servings.

**Per serving:** *234 cal., 22 g pro., 18 g carbo., 8 g total fat (1 g sat. fat), 40 mg cholesterol, 1 g dietary fiber, 289 mg sodium. Daily Value: 56% vit. C, 23% folate, 18% thiamine, 12% iron, 35% potassium.*

# Orange-Sauced Fish with Linguine

*To speed up dinner preparation, cook the fish and sauce in the microwave while simmering the pasta on the range top.*

| | |
|---|---|
| 4 | 4-ounce frozen fish fillets |
| ½ | cup water |
| ¼ | cup frozen Florida Orange Juice *Concentrate*, thawed |
| 2 | teaspoons cornstarch |
| 1 | teaspoon instant chicken bouillon granules |
| ½ | teaspoon finely shredded Florida Orange Peel |
| ¼ | teaspoon dry mustard |
| ¼ | teaspoon dried dillweed |
| 1 | Florida Orange, peeled, sectioned, and seeded |
| 2 | tablespoons sliced green onion |
| 4 | ounces spinach or plain linguine or fettuccine, cooked and drained |

Thaw fish. Place thawed fish in a microwave-safe shallow baking dish. Arrange with thicker portions toward the outer edges of the dish for more even cooking. Turn under any thin portions of fish to obtain an even thickness.

Cover with vented microwave-safe plastic wrap. Micro-cook on 100% power (high) for 4 to 7 minutes or until fish begins to flake easily with a fork, giving the dish a half turn once. Set aside.

For sauce, in a 2-cup microwave-safe measure combine water, thawed orange juice concentrate, cornstarch, bouillon granules, orange peel, mustard, and dillweed.

Micro-cook, uncovered, on high for 2 to 3 minutes or until thickened and bubbly, stirring every minute until slightly thickened, then every 30 seconds. Stir in the orange sections and green onion. Cook, uncovered, on high for 30 seconds more.

To serve, place fish on top of pasta on 4 serving plates; spoon orange sauce over fish. Makes 4 servings.

**Per serving (with pasta):** *250 cal., 24 g pro., 34 g carbo., 1 g total fat (0 g sat. fat), 40 mg cholesterol, 3 g dietary fiber, 314 mg sodium. Daily Value: 50% vit. C, 31% folate, 21% thiamine, 11% riboflavin, 28% niacin, 37% potassium.*

olate, sometimes called folic acid or folacin, is a B vitamin that's important for normal cell multiplication. Women of childbearing age who consume adequate amounts of folate may reduce the incidence of certain birth defects. Florida Orange Juice is an excellent source of folate and the most commonly consumed source of this vitamin.

← **Orange-Sauced Fish with Linguine**

## Shrimp and Vegetable Stir-Fry

*For a delicious change of taste, orange juice flavors this dish instead of soy sauce.*

| | |
|---|---|
| ½ | cup water |
| ⅓ | cup frozen Florida Orange Juice *Concentrate,* thawed |
| 2 | tablespoons honey |
| 2 | teaspoons cornstarch |
| 1¼ | teaspoons Dijon-style mustard |
| ¼ | teaspoon dried thyme, crushed Nonstick spray coating |
| 2 | cups bias-sliced yellow summer squash |
| 2 | green onions, bias sliced into 1-inch pieces |
| 1 | tablespoon olive oil or cooking oil |
| 12 | ounces peeled and deveined shrimp (about 1 pound in shells) |
| 1 | cup fresh pea pods, strings removed, or one 6-ounce package frozen pea pods, thawed |
| 1 | 8-ounce can sliced water chestnuts, drained |
| 2 | cups hot cooked rice |

For sauce, in a small bowl combine the water, thawed orange juice concentrate, honey, cornstarch, mustard, and thyme. Set the mixture aside.

Spray an unheated wok or large skillet with nonstick coating. Preheat over medium heat. Stir-fry squash and green onions about 3 minutes or until squash is crisp-tender. Remove vegetables from wok or skillet.

Add oil to wok. Stir-fry shrimp for 2 to 3 minutes or until pink. Push shrimp from center of wok.

Stir sauce; pour into center of wok. Cook and stir until thickened and bubbly. Return vegetables to wok; add pea pods and water chestnuts. Toss shrimp and vegetables gently to coat with sauce. Cook and stir about 1 minute or until mixture is heated through. Serve immediately over rice. Makes 4 servings.

**Per serving (with rice):** *358 cal., 20 g pro., 60 g carbo., 5 g total fat (1 g sat. fat), 125 mg cholesterol, 4 g dietary fiber, 210 mg sodium. Daily Value: 69% vit. C, 41% folate, 52% thiamine, 10% riboflavin, 31% niacin, 10% calcium, 33% iron, 30% potassium.*

Nonstick spray coating is a convenient way to reduce fat in cooking. When using the spray, follow these pointers:
• Spray nonstick coating on an unheated pan, as the coating can burn or smoke if it is sprayed onto hot surfaces.
• Preheat sprayed pans over medium, instead of high, heat.
• Use spray sparingly.
• Hold the pan over the sink, so the spray doesn't hit the floor or countertop and make it slippery.

# Grilled Salmon and Vegetables with Orange-Basil Sauce

*Brushing the salmon and vegetables with the orange sauce heightens their flavor and keeps them moist.*

| | |
|---|---|
| 1 | 1½-pound boneless, skinless fresh or frozen salmon fillet |
| ¼ | cup frozen Florida Orange Juice Concentrate, thawed |
| 3 | tablespoons olive oil or cooking oil |
| 2 | tablespoons snipped fresh basil or 2 teaspoons dried basil, crushed |
| 2 | tablespoons water |
| 1 | tablespoon snipped fresh mint or tarragon or 1 teaspoon dried mint or tarragon, crushed |
| 1 | tablespoon Worcestershire sauce |
| 2 | cloves garlic, minced |
| 3 | small zucchini and/or yellow summer squash, halved lengthwise |
| 6 | ounces fettuccine or linguine, cooked and drained |

Thaw fish, if frozen. For sauce, in a bowl combine thawed orange juice concentrate, oil, basil, water, mint or tarragon, Worcestershire sauce, and garlic.

Rinse salmon; brush with sauce. Brush a wire grill basket with additional oil. Place salmon in basket, tucking under thin ends to make an even thickness. Measure fillet thickness. Close basket.

Place grill basket on an uncovered grill directly over *medium-hot* coals. Place zucchini on grill rack next to basket. Grill until salmon begins to flake easily with a fork and zucchini is tender. Allow 4 to 6 minutes per ½-inch thickness of fish and 5 to 6 minutes for zucchini or squash. During cooking, brush fish and vegetables often with sauce and turn squash occasionally. (If salmon is more than 1 inch thick, turn halfway through grilling.) Serve with fettuccine or linguine. Makes 6 servings.

**Per serving (with pasta):** *382 cal., 28 g pro., 29 g carbo., 17 g total fat (3 g sat. fat), 80 mg cholesterol, 2 g dietary fiber, 88 mg sodium. Daily Value: 27% vit. C, 11% vit. A, 22% folate, 49% thiamine, 22% riboflavin, 57% niacin, 12% iron, 32% potassium.*

# Grilled Orange-Marinated Steak

| | |
|---|---|
| 1 | 1- to 1½-pound beef sirloin steak, cut 1 inch thick |
| ¾ | cup Citrus Base (see recipe, page 43) Florida Orange Slices |

Place meat in a plastic bag set in a shallow dish; add Citrus Base. Close bag. Marinate meat in the refrigerator overnight, turning bag occasionally. Remove meat from bag. Discard marinade.

Place meat on the grill rack of an uncovered grill. Grill directly over *medium* coals, turning once, allowing 12 to 15 minutes for medium. Garnish with orange slices. Makes 4 to 6 servings.

**Per serving:** *354 cal., 22 g pro., 18 g carbo., 21 g total fat (6 g sat. fat), 70 mg cholesterol, 1 g dietary fiber, 292 mg sodium. Daily Value: 56% vit. C, 26% folate, 19% thiamine, 21% riboflavin, 26% niacin, 21% iron, 29% potassium.*

# Marinated Flank Steak with Citrus Salsa

*To warm tortillas, stack them and wrap in foil. Heat in a 350° oven for 10 minutes.*

| | |
|---|---|
| ³⁄₄ | **cup frozen Florida Orange Juice or Grapefruit Juice *Concentrate*, thawed** |
| 1 | **or 2 jalapeño peppers, seeded and finely chopped** |
| 1 | **teaspoon black pepper** |
| 1 | **teaspoon paprika** |
| ½ | **cup water** |
| 1 | **1- to 1½-pound beef flank steak** |
| ¼ | **cup thinly sliced green onions** |
| 2 | **tablespoons snipped parsley** |
| 1 | **tablespoon lime juice** |
| | **Dash salt** |
| 2 | **Florida Oranges, peeled, seeded, and chopped** |
| 1 | **Florida Grapefruit, peeled, seeded, and chopped** |
| | **Jalapeño peppers (optional)** |
| 1 | **Florida Grapefruit, sliced (optional)** |
| 6 | **6- to 7-inch flour tortillas, warmed** |

For marinade, in a small bowl combine thawed orange or grapefruit juice concentrate, finely chopped jalapeño pepper, black pepper, and paprika. Reserve *2 tablespoons* of the mixture for salsa. Add the water to remaining mixture.

Score steak by making shallow cuts at 1-inch intervals diagonally across steak in a diamond pattern. Repeat on second side. Place in a plastic bag set in a shallow dish. Pour marinade over steak; close bag. Marinate in the refrigerator for 2 to 24 hours; turn bag occasionally.

For salsa, in a nonmetallic bowl stir together the *2 tablespoons* juice concentrate mixture, the onions, parsley, lime juice, and salt. Add chopped oranges and grapefruit; stir gently. Cover and chill at least 30 minutes to blend flavors.

← **Marinated Flank Steak with Citrus Salsa**

Remove meat from bag. Discard marinade. Place meat on the grill rack of an uncovered grill. Grill directly over *medium* coals, turning once, allowing 12 to 14 minutes for medium-rare.

Thinly slice meat. If desired, garnish with jalapeños and grapefruit slices. Serve with salsa and warmed tortillas. Makes 6 servings.

**To broil:** Place steak on the unheated rack of a broiler pan. Broil 3 inches from heat for 6 minutes. Turn and broil 7 to 8 minutes more for medium-rare. Serve as above.

**Per serving:** *298 cal., 19 g pro., 37 g carbo., 8 g total fat (3 g sat. fat), 38 mg cholesterol, 3 g dietary fiber, 233 mg sodium. Daily Value: 90% vit. C, 39% folate, 37% thiamine, 21% riboflavin, 34% niacin, 10% calcium, 20% iron, 32% potassium.*

Keep a touch of Florida sunshine on hand in your refrigerator for nutritious snacks and easy garnishes. Store Florida Citrus Fruit, including Grapefruit, Oranges, Tangerines, Temple Oranges, and Tangelos, in the crisper section for up to three weeks.

## Orange-Ginger-Glazed Barbecued Ribs

| | |
|---|---|
| 4 | pounds pork loin back ribs or meaty pork spareribs |
| 3/4 | cup frozen Florida Orange Juice Concentrate, thawed |
| 1/3 | cup sliced green onions |
| 2 | teaspoons grated fresh gingerroot |
| 1 | teaspoon Worcestershire sauce |
| 2 | cloves garlic, minced |
| 1/4 | teaspoon pepper |
| 4 | Florida Oranges, peeled, thinly sliced, and seeded |

Cut the ribs into serving-size pieces. For barbecue sauce, in a bowl combine thawed orange juice concentrate, onions, gingerroot, Worcestershire sauce, garlic, and pepper.

In a covered grill arrange *medium-hot* coals around a drip pan. Test for *medium* heat above the pan. Place ribs on the grill rack over the drip pan. Cover and grill for 1¼ to 1½ hours or until ribs are tender and no pink remains, brushing occasionally with the barbecue sauce the last 10 minutes of grilling. Serve with orange slices. Makes 6 servings.

**To roast:** Place ribs, bone side down, on a rack in a shallow pan. Roast in a 350° oven for 1 hour. Brush with the sauce, then roast 30 to 45 minutes more or until no pink remains, brushing occasionally with the sauce.

**Per serving:** *446 cal., 25 g pro., 24 g carbo., 28 g total fat (10 g sat. fat), 111 mg cholesterol, 3 g dietary fiber, 106 mg sodium. Daily Value: 144% vit. C, 38% folate, 58% thiamine, 21% riboflavin, 30% niacin, 13% calcium, 11% iron, 34% potassium.*

## Citrus Corned Beef Dinner

| | |
|---|---|
| 1 | 2½-pound corned beef brisket |
| 3/4 | cup frozen Florida Orange Juice Concentrate, thawed |
| 1 | teaspoon whole black peppers |
| 2 | bay leaves |
| 2 | cloves garlic, minced |
| 4 | juniper berries (optional) |
| 3 | medium potatoes, peeled and quartered |
| 6 | medium carrots, quartered |
| 8 | ounces whole fresh mushrooms |
| 1 | medium onion, sliced |
| 1 | teaspoon dried basil, crushed |
| 2/3 | cup light or regular dairy sour cream |
| 1 | to 2 teaspoons brown mustard or Dijon-style mustard |

Trim fat from meat. Place in a 4-quart Dutch oven; add juices and spices from meat package. Add water to nearly cover meat. Reserve and refrigerate *1 tablespoon* of the thawed orange juice concentrate. Add remaining orange juice concentrate, the black peppers, bay leaves, garlic, and juniper berries, if desired, to the Dutch oven. Bring to boiling; reduce heat. Cover and simmer about 2 hours or until meat is almost tender.

Add vegetables and basil. Return to boiling; reduce heat. Cover and simmer for 30 to 40 minutes more or until vegetables are tender. Discard bay leaves. Remove meat and vegetables to serving platter. For sauce, stir together sour cream, the reserved concentrate, and mustard. Pass sauce with meat. Serves 6.

**Per serving:** *318 cal., 15 g pro., 38 g carbo., 12 g total fat (3 g sat. fat), 58 mg cholesterol, 4 g dietary fiber, 632 mg sodium. Daily Value: 69% vit. C, 254% vit. A, 39% folate, 27% thiamine, 28% riboflavin, 37% niacin, 15% iron, 45% potassium.*

# Orange-Spice Pot Roast

*Traditional pot roast is even more savory when cooked in an orange juice mixture.*

| | |
|---|---|
| 1 | **2- to 2½-pound boneless beef chuck arm pot roast** |
| | **Nonstick spray coating** |
| 3 | **inches stick cinnamon, broken** |
| 6 | **whole cloves** |
| 3 | **medium sweet potatoes (about 1 pound) or one 18-ounce can vacuum-packed sweet potatoes, drained** |
| 1 | **pound turnips or rutabagas, peeled and cut into 1-inch pieces** |
| 1 | **medium onion, sliced and separated into rings** |
| 3 | **tablespoons quick-cooking tapioca** |
| ⅓ | **cup frozen Florida Orange Juice Concentrate, thawed** |
| ¼ | **cup light corn syrup** |
| ½ | **teaspoon salt** |

Trim as much fat as possible from roast. If necessary, cut the roast to fit into a 3½- or 4-quart electric crockery cooker. Spray an unheated large skillet with nonstick coating. Heat skillet over medium heat. Brown roast on all sides in the hot skillet.

Place cinnamon and cloves on a double thickness of 100% cotton cheesecloth. Gather up the edges and tie with a string. Place the spices in the crockery cooker.

If using fresh sweet potatoes, wash, peel, and cut off woody portions and ends. Cut sweet potatoes into quarters. Place fresh sweet potatoes in crockery cooker. (If using canned sweet potatoes, do not add them to cooker at this point.) Add turnips and onion; sprinkle tapioca over vegetables.

In a small bowl stir together thawed orange juice concentrate, corn syrup, and salt; pour over vegetables in cooker. Place roast atop vegetables. (If using canned sweet potatoes, place them atop roast.)

Cover and cook on the low-heat setting for 10 to 12 hours or on the high-heat setting for 5 to 6 hours.

Transfer roast and vegetables to a serving platter. Skim fat from cooking juices, if necessary. Discard spice bag. Pass the cooking juices with the meat. Makes 6 servings.

**Per serving:** *429 cal., 40 g pro., 44 g carbo., 10 g total fat (3 g sat. fat), 114 mg cholesterol, 4 g dietary fiber, 318 mg sodium. Daily Value: 53% vit. C, 167% vit. A, 31% folate, 21% thiamine, 39% riboflavin, 38% niacin, 34% iron, 35% potassium.*

# Spicy Stir-Fried Pork

*Stir-frying is ideal for today's lifestyle, because it's fast, uses little fat, and doesn't require special equipment. (You can use a large skillet if you don't have a wok.)*

| | |
|---|---|
| 12 | ounces pork tenderloin or boneless pork sirloin |
| ½ | cup reduced-sodium chicken broth |
| ⅓ | cup frozen Florida Orange Juice *Concentrate,* thawed |
| 2 | tablespoons soy sauce |
| 1 | tablespoon cornstarch |
| 1 | tablespoon brown sugar |
| ¼ | to ½ teaspoon crushed red pepper |
| 1 | tablespoon olive oil or cooking oil |
| 2 | cloves garlic, minced |
| 2 | teaspoons grated fresh gingerroot |
| 1 | large red or green sweet pepper, cut into thin strips |
| 1 | cup sliced onion |
| 2 | cups hot cooked rice or pasta |

Trim fat from pork, if necessary. Partially freeze pork. Thinly slice across the grain into bite-size strips.

For sauce, in a small bowl stir together chicken broth, thawed orange juice concentrate, soy sauce, cornstarch, brown sugar, and crushed red pepper. Set aside.

Pour oil into a wok or 12-inch skillet. Preheat over medium-high heat. Stir-fry garlic and gingerroot for 15 seconds. Add sweet pepper strips and onion. Stir-fry about 3 minutes or until vegetables are crisp-tender. Remove vegetables from wok.

Add the pork to the wok. Stir-fry for 2 to 3 minutes or until pork is no longer pink. Push pork from center of wok. Stir sauce; pour into center of wok. Cook and stir until thickened and bubbly. Return vegetables to wok. Stir meat and vegetables together to coat with sauce. Cook and stir for 1 to 2 minutes or until heated through. Serve immediately over hot cooked rice or pasta. Makes 4 servings.

**Per serving (with rice):** *417 cal., 26 g pro., 47 g carbo., 13 g total fat (4 g sat. fat), 67 mg cholesterol, 2 g dietary fiber, 646 mg sodium. Daily Value: 78% vit. C, 14% vit. A, 30% folate, 70% thiamine, 23% riboflavin, 51% niacin, 18% iron, 29% potassium.*

# Pork with Orange-Basil Pesto

*This deliciously nippy pesto is lower in fat than typical pestos, because orange juice concentrate replaces some of the oil, Parmesan cheese, and nuts.*

| | |
|---|---|
| ⅓ | cup frozen Florida Orange Juice *Concentrate,* thawed |
| 1 | cup firmly packed fresh basil leaves |
| ½ | cup firmly packed fresh parsley sprigs |
| ¼ | cup firmly packed fresh mint leaves |
| 1 | large clove garlic, quartered |
| ¼ | cup grated Parmesan cheese |
| 2 | tablespoons olive oil or cooking oil |
| | Nonstick spray coating |
| 4 | boneless pork loin chops, cut ¾ inch thick |
| 6 | ounces fettuccine or linguine, cooked and drained |
| 4 | Florida Orange Slices |

Set aside *1 tablespoon* of the thawed orange juice concentrate for the pork.

For pesto, in a blender container or food processor bowl combine basil, parsley, mint, and garlic. Add remaining orange juice concentrate, Parmesan cheese, and oil. Cover and blend or process with on-and-off turns until mixture is well blended. Divide mixture into 2 portions (about ⅓ cup each) and place in small, airtight containers. Refrigerate up to 1 or 2 days or freeze up to 1 month.

Spray an unheated heavy large skillet with nonstick coating. Heat over medium heat. Add pork chops and panbroil for 3 to 4 minutes. Turn chops and brush with the reserved 1 tablespoon orange juice. Cook for 3 to 4 minutes more or until slightly pink in center and juices run clear.

To serve, place pork chops and hot cooked pasta on 4 dinner plates. Using one container of the pesto, top each serving with about *1 tablespoon.* Garnish with orange slices. Makes 4 servings.

**Per serving:** *407 cal., 31 g pro., 41 g carbo., 13 g total fat (4 g sat. fat), 80 mg cholesterol, 2 g dietary fiber, 103 mg sodium. Daily Value: 45% vit. C, 24% folate, 95% thiamine, 36% riboflavin, 54% niacin, 11% calcium, 19% iron, 32% potassium.*

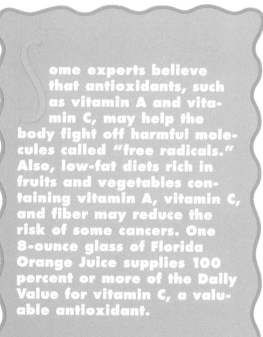

ome experts believe that antioxidants, such as vitamin A and vitamin C, may help the body fight off harmful molecules called "free radicals." Also, low-fat diets rich in fruits and vegetables containing vitamin A, vitamin C, and fiber may reduce the risk of some cancers. One 8-ounce glass of Florida Orange Juice supplies 100 percent or more of the Daily Value for vitamin C, a valuable antioxidant.

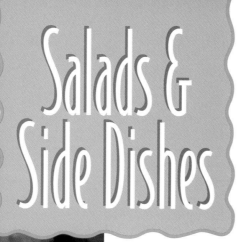

# Salads & Side Dishes

With Florida Citrus as a featured player, even the simplest of salads and side dishes becomes a show-stopper. For fast, nutritious meals, rely on easy main-dish salads, such as Bow-Tie Pasta and Pork Salad, pictured at left. Or, as a complement to an entrée, prepare the sunny Singapore Slaw, Skillet Sweet Potatoes, or Asparagus with Zesty Orange Sauce. The special section of zippy salad dressings provides additional ideas.

← **Bow-Tie Pasta and Pork Salad**
(see recipe, page 27)

# Grapefruit and Black Bean Salad

*Florida Grapefruit Juice Concentrate makes a full-bodied base for this tangy, fat-free salad dressing. Use the remaining concentrate to mix up a beverage. See the tip on page 59.*

|       | Lettuce leaves |
|-------|----------------|
| 2     | Florida Grapefruit, peeled, thinly sliced, and seeded |
| 1     | 15-ounce can black beans, rinsed and drained |
| 1     | medium cucumber, halved lengthwise and sliced |
| 1     | cup cubed canned papaya, drained |
| 2     | ounces reduced-fat Monterey Jack cheese, cut into ¼-inch cubes |
| ⅓     | cup frozen Florida Grapefruit Juice *Concentrate*, thawed |
| ¼     | cup water |
| 2     | tablespoons snipped fresh cilantro |
| 2     | teaspoons honey |
| ¼     | teaspoon ground cumin |

Line 4 salad plates with lettuce. Arrange grapefruit slices on plates. Arrange beans, cucumber, and papaya in mounds on lettuce. Sprinkle with cheese.

For dressing, in a screw-top jar combine thawed grapefruit juice concentrate, water, cilantro, honey, and cumin. Cover and shake well. Drizzle some of the dressing over the salads. Pass remaining dressing. Makes 4 main-dish servings.

**Per serving:** *219 cal., 13 g pro., 41 g carbo., 4 g total fat (2 g sat. fat), 10 mg cholesterol, 3 g dietary fiber, 384 mg sodium. Daily Value: 167% vit. C, 12% vit. A, 23% folate, 20% thiamine, 12% riboflavin, 22% calcium, 14% iron, 35% potassium.*

# Curried Chicken and Fruit Salad

*Don't waste a drop of Florida sunshine! When sectioning the oranges, work over a bowl to catch the sweet juices. See page 78 for easy directions for sectioning citrus fruit.*

| | |
|-------|---|
| ¾     | cup tiny shell macaroni |
| 3     | Florida Oranges |
| 1½    | cups halved seedless green or red grapes |
| 1⅓    | cups chopped cooked chicken, turkey, or lean beef (about 7 ounces) |
| 1     | 8-ounce carton lemon low-fat yogurt |
| ¼     | cup dairy sour cream |
| 2     | tablespoons milk |
| 1     | to 2 teaspoons curry powder |

Cook pasta according to package directions. Drain pasta. Rinse with cold water; drain well.

Meanwhile, peel, section, and seed oranges, reserving the juices. In a large salad bowl toss together orange sections and juice, cooked pasta, grapes, and poultry or beef.

For dressing, in a small mixing bowl stir together lemon yogurt, sour cream, milk, and curry powder. Pour dressing over salad mixture. Toss lightly to coat. Cover and chill for 4 to 24 hours. Before serving, if necessary, stir in additional *milk* to moisten. Makes 4 main-dish servings.

**Per serving:** *353 cal., 23 g pro., 52 g carbo., 7 g total fat (3 g sat. fat), 52 mg cholesterol, 4 g dietary fiber, 85 mg sodium. Daily Value: 97% vit. C, 17% folate, 23% thiamine, 22% riboflavin, 52% niacin, 22% calcium, 11% iron, 29% potassium.*

# Bow-Tie Pasta and Pork Salad

*Whip together this easy meal using meat from the deli section of the supermarket or leftover roast. Pictured on pages 24–25.*

2   cups bow-tie pasta or mostaccioli
2   cups cooked pork, chicken, turkey, or beef
    cut into bite-size strips
4   small Florida Oranges, Tangerines,
    or Tangelos, peeled, sectioned, and seeded
¾   cup sliced red onion separated into rings
½   cup fat-free mayonnaise dressing or
    salad dressing
⅓   cup frozen Florida Orange Juice
    *Concentrate*, thawed
    Dash paprika
    Fresh spinach leaves
¼   cup sliced pitted ripe olives (optional)

Cook pasta according to package directions. Drain pasta. Quickly chill pasta by placing in a colander in a large bowl of ice water for a few minutes. Drain well. In a large salad bowl toss together meat strips, citrus sections, and onion. Add pasta; toss gently.

For dressing, in a small mixing bowl stir together mayonnaise dressing, thawed orange juice concentrate, and paprika. Pour dressing over salad mixture; toss gently.

To serve, line 4 dinner plates with spinach; spoon salad mixture atop spinach. If desired, top with olives. Makes 4 main-dish servings.

**Per serving:** *490 cal., 30 g pro., 69 g carbo., 12 g total fat (4 g sat. fat), 67 mg cholesterol, 2 g dietary fiber, 329 mg sodium. Daily Value: 110% vit. C, 37% vit. A, 63% folate, 79% thiamine, 32% riboflavin, 40% niacin, 10% calcium, 27% iron, 37% potassium.*

I n addition to superb oranges and grapefruit, Florida also produces delicious specialty fruit. Among them is the tangerine, a type of mandarin orange, which has a sweet, yet slightly tart flavor. Tangerines are sometimes called the "zipper-skin fruit" because of their easy-to-remove peel. Temple oranges, a cross between the orange and the tangerine, have a sweet, rich flavor similar to oranges. They are very juicy, which makes them great for juicing. Tangelos, a cross between the tangerine and the grapefruit, have a tart-sweet flavor that's closer to the flavor of tangerines than grapefruit.

# Seafood Salad with Oranges

*Cartwheel citrus slices lend stylish pizzazz to this salad plate. To make the cartwheels, use a zester to etch a strip down the side of the whole fruit from the stem end to the blossom end. Then etch a strip on the opposite side of the fruit. Repeat at regular intervals around the fruit, then slice the fruit.*

|   | Chinese cabbage leaves |
|---|---|
| 4 | cups shredded romaine or iceberg lettuce |
| 2 | 8-ounce packages frozen, crab-flavored fish pieces, thawed and cut into 1-inch pieces, or two 8-ounce packages frozen, peeled, cooked shrimp, thawed |
| 3 | Florida Oranges, peeled, sectioned, and seeded |
| 1 | small avocado, halved, seeded, peeled, and sliced (optional) |
| 1/2 | cup Thousand Island Dressing or bottled Thousand Island salad dressing |
|   | Florida Orange Slices (optional) |
|   | Lime slices (optional) |
|   | Fresh thyme sprigs (optional) |

Line 4 salad plates with Chinese cabbage leaves. Pile shredded romaine or iceberg lettuce in the center of each plate.

Place crab-flavored fish pieces or shrimp atop the shredded romaine. Arrange orange sections and, if desired, avocado slices on the sides of each salad. Spoon dressing over salads. If desired, garnish with orange and lime slices and thyme. Serve at once. Makes 4 main-dish servings.

**Thousand Island Dressing:** In a small mixing bowl combine ½ cup *reduced-calorie mayonnaise* or *salad dressing* and 2 tablespoons *chili sauce*. Stir in 1 tablespoon finely chopped *pimiento-stuffed olives*, 1 tablespoon finely chopped *green* or *red sweet pepper*, 1 tablespoon finely chopped *onion*, ½ teaspoon *Worcestershire sauce* or *prepared horseradish* (if desired), and ½ *hard-cooked egg*, finely chopped. Before serving, if necessary, stir in 2 to 3 teaspoons *milk* to make dressing the desired consistency. Cover and store dressing in the refrigerator. Makes ¾ cup.

*Per serving: 323 cal., 16 g pro., 37 g carbo., 14 g total fat (3 g sat. fat), 33 mg cholesterol, 5 g dietary fiber, 887 mg sodium. Daily Value: 126% vit. C, 27% vit. A, 73% folate, 42% thiamine, 24% riboflavin, 12% niacin, 11% calcium, 14% iron, 34% potassium.*

# Tangelo-Tuna Salad

*Tote a portion of this salad to the office for a lunch that's as healthful as it is tasty.*

|   |   |
|---|---|
| 1 | cup tiny bow-tie pasta, tiny shell macaroni, or ditalini pasta |
| 3 | Florida Tangelos, Tangerines, or Temple Oranges, peeled, seeded, and chopped |
| 1 | cup chopped red, yellow, or green sweet pepper |
| 1 | cup halved seedless green or red grapes |
| 1/4 | cup sliced green onions |
| 3 | tablespoons snipped parsley |
| 1/2 | cup plain fat-free yogurt |
| 2 | tablespoons fat-free mayonnaise dressing or salad dressing |
| 2 | tablespoons mango chutney, finely chopped |
| 2 | tablespoons Florida Tangelo, Tangerine, or Temple Orange Juice |
| 1 | 9 1/4-ounce can chunk white tuna (water pack), drained and broken into chunks Lettuce leaves Florida Tangelo, Tangerine, or Temple Orange Slices |

Cook pasta according to package directions. Drain pasta. Rinse with cold water; drain well. In a large bowl toss together the chopped tangelos, sweet pepper, grapes, green onions, and parsley.

For dressing, in a small bowl stir together yogurt, mayonnaise dressing, and chutney. Stir in the tangelo juice.

Spoon dressing over fruit mixture and toss to coat. Gently stir in the tuna and cooked pasta. Season to taste with salt. Cover and chill at least 30 minutes or up to 6 hours. Serve on lettuce and garnish with tangelo slices. Makes 4 main-dish servings.

**Per serving:** *287 cal., 21 g pro., 49 g carbo., 1 g total fat (0 g sat. fat), 18 mg cholesterol, 2 g dietary fiber, 367 mg sodium. Daily Value: 132% vit. C, 30% vit. A, 19% folate, 17% thiamine, 14% riboflavin, 61% niacin, 12% calcium, 16% iron, 24% potassium.*

Look for Florida specialty fruit in the market at various times of the year. Tangerines are usually available September through April. Temple oranges are generally found in the stores January through March, while tangelos are available from October through February. Whenever these fruits are on the market, they are ripe and ready to enjoy.

# Prune and Citrus Salad

*The flavors of this colorful salad are a perfect complement to roast pork or turkey.*

| | |
|---|---|
| 2 | Florida Oranges |
| 2 | Florida Grapefruit |
| | Florida Orange Juice |
| 8 | pitted prunes, cut in half |
| 1 | tablespoon snipped fresh mint or ½ teaspoon dried mint, crushed |
| 1 | tablespoon honey |
| | Lettuce leaves |

Finely shred enough orange peel from one of the oranges to equal *1 teaspoon*; set orange peel aside. Working over a mixing bowl to catch the juices, peel, section, and seed the oranges and the grapefruit. Set aside the fruit sections. Transfer the reserved juices to a measuring cup. Add enough additional orange juice to equal ⅓ *cup*.

In a small saucepan combine the juice mixture and the prunes. Bring to boiling; remove from heat. Stir in the orange peel, mint, and honey. Transfer the mixture to a bowl. Gently stir in the orange and grapefruit sections. Cover and chill for 2 to 24 hours.

To serve, line 4 salad bowls with lettuce. Using a slotted spoon, transfer fruit mixture to the bowls. Makes 4 side-dish servings.

**Per serving:** *133 cal., 2 g pro., 34 g carbo., 0 g total fat (0 g sat. fat), 0 mg cholesterol, 5 g dietary fiber, 3 mg sodium. Daily Value: 128% vit. C, 21% folate, 14% thiamine, 23% potassium.*

# Winter Fruits with Balsamic Vinaigrette

*A blend of tangy orange juice and sweet, delicate balsamic vinegar, this delightful dressing is also good on tossed salads.*

| | |
|---|---|
| ¼ | cup Florida Orange Juice |
| ¼ | cup salad oil |
| 3 | tablespoons balsamic vinegar |
| 1 | tablespoon honey |
| ⅛ | teaspoon cracked pepper |
| 2 | Florida Red Grapefruit |
| 1 | Florida Orange |
| 2 | medium pears |
| 2 | teaspoons lemon juice |
| 1 | head red or green leaf lettuce |
| 1 | cup seedless red and/or green grapes |

For dressing, to a blender container or food processor bowl add orange juice, salad oil, vinegar, honey, and pepper. Cover and blend or process until combined. Cover and chill until serving time.

Peel grapefruit and orange. Section grapefruit and cut orange crosswise into 8 slices; remove seeds. Core pears and cut into wedges. Brush pears with lemon juice.

Line a large platter with lettuce leaves. Arrange grapefruit sections, orange slices, pear wedges, and grapes atop lettuce. Cover the platter with plastic wrap and chill for up to 4 hours. Before serving, drizzle with dressing. Makes 8 side-dish servings.

**Per serving:** *144 cal., 1 g pro., 21 g carbo., 7 g total fat (1 g sat. fat), 0 mg cholesterol, 3 g dietary fiber, 5 mg sodium. Daily Value: 77% vit. C, 11% vit. A, 18% folate, 15% potassium.*

# Singapore Slaw

*For a practically fat-free salad, omit the peanuts or pass them for diners to sprinkle on their salads as they wish.*

| | |
|---|---|
| 3 | cups shredded cabbage or preshredded coleslaw mix (contains cabbage and carrots) |
| 1½ | cups peeled jicama cut into thin, bite-size strips |
| 4 | Florida Oranges, peeled, sectioned, and seeded |
| ½ | of a medium red, green, or yellow sweet pepper, cut into thin bite-size strips |
| 1 | small red onion, thinly sliced and separated into rings |
| 2 | tablespoons snipped fresh cilantro or parsley |
| 1 | teaspoon finely shredded Florida Orange Peel |
| ¼ | cup Florida Orange Juice |
| 1 | tablespoon rice vinegar or lemon juice |
| 2 | teaspoons soy sauce |
| 1 | teaspoon toasted sesame oil |
| 2 | tablespoons dry roasted peanuts |

In a large salad bowl combine cabbage, jicama, orange sections, pepper strips, onion, and cilantro. Cover and chill up to 4 hours.

For dressing, in a screw-top jar combine orange peel, orange juice, vinegar, soy sauce, and sesame oil. Cover and shake well; pour over the salad mixture. Toss lightly to coat. Sprinkle with peanuts. Makes 6 to 8 side-dish servings.

**Per serving:** *103 cal., 3 g pro., 19 g carbo., 3 g total fat (0 g sat. fat), 0 mg cholesterol, 5 g dietary fiber, 150 mg sodium. Daily Value: 134% vit. C, 33% folate, 17% thiamine, 19% potassium.*

Women of childbearing age, female athletes, and some vegetarians are at increased risk of becoming iron deficient. Adding Florida Citrus to meals may help. The ascorbic acid in citrus fruit helps the body absorb more iron from nonmeat foods. By drinking Florida Orange or Grapefruit Juice with a meal, you may be helping your body obtain the usable iron it needs from other foods in your diet.

← Singapore Slaw

# Fruit Salad with Grapefruit-Poppy Seed Dressing

*If you're making this salad ahead, brush a little grapefruit juice on the avocado slices to prevent darkening.*

|   | Lettuce leaves |
|---|---|
|   | Shredded fresh spinach and/or lettuce |
| 2 | Florida Red Grapefruit, peeled, sectioned, and seeded |
| 2 | Florida White Grapefruit, peeled, sectioned, and seeded |
| 2 | cups strawberries, sliced or halved |
| 2 | medium avocados, halved, seeded, peeled, and sliced |
| 1 | small red onion, thinly sliced and separated into rings |

Line a platter with lettuce leaves. Top with shredded spinach or lettuce. Arrange red and white grapefruit sections, strawberries, and avocados on lettuce. Sprinkle red onion rings on top of fruit. Serve with Grapefruit-Poppy Seed Dressing (see recipe below). Store remaining dressing, covered, in the refrigerator. Makes 8 side-dish servings.

**Per serving (without dressing):** *137 cal., 2 g pro., 17 g carbo., 8 g total fat (1 g sat. fat), 0 mg cholesterol, 4 g dietary fiber, 9 mg sodium. Daily Value: 116% vit. C, 40% folate, 12% thiamine, 10% riboflavin, 11% niacin, 30% potassium.*

**Grapefruit-Poppy Seed Dressing:** In a mixing bowl stir together 1 cup *honey*, 1 teaspoon finely shredded *Florida Grapefruit Peel*, 1 cup *Florida Grapefruit Juice*, ½ teaspoon *salt*, and ½ teaspoon *ground nutmeg*. Gradually beat in 1¼ cups *salad oil*. Stir in 1½ teaspoons *poppy seed*. Transfer to a screw-top jar; cover and chill until serving time. Shake well before using. Serve over fruit or tossed salads. Makes 3 cups.

**Per tablespoon:** *74 cal., 0 g pro., 6 g carbo., 6 g total fat (0 g sat. fat), 0 mg cholesterol, 0 g dietary fiber, 23 mg sodium. Daily Value: none.*

For a healthful diet, nutritionists recommend that we consume no more than 30 percent of our daily calories from fat.

To calculate the percentage of calories from fat for a given day, multiply the total fat intake for that day (in grams) times 9. Divide this number by the day's total calorie intake. Then multiply this number by 100. The result is the percentage of calories from fat.

# Citrus Platter with Raspberry Sauce

*Orange and grapefruit sections drizzled with a ruby-red, fat-free sauce makes the perfect salad for a celebration dinner.*

- 1    12-ounce package frozen lightly sweetened red raspberries, thawed
- 2    tablespoons sugar
- 1    tablespoon cornstarch
- 1/8  teaspoon ground mace
- 2    teaspoons vanilla
- 4    Florida Red and/or White Grapefruit, peeled, sectioned, and seeded
- 7    Florida Oranges, peeled, sectioned, and seeded
       Fresh mint sprigs (optional)

For sauce, sieve the thawed raspberries and discard the seeds. Add water to raspberry purée to make 1¼ cups. In a small saucepan combine the raspberry purée, sugar, cornstarch, and mace. Cook and stir over medium heat until thickened and bubbly. Cook and stir 2 minutes more. Remove from heat. Stir in vanilla. Cover and chill about 2 hours.

Arrange grapefruit and orange sections on a platter. Cover and chill until serving time. To serve, drizzle the chilled raspberry sauce over the fruit. If desired, garnish with fresh mint sprigs. Makes 8 side-dish servings.

**Per serving:** *158 cal., 2 g pro., 40 g carbo., 0 g total fat (0 g sat. fat), 0 mg cholesterol, 7 g dietary fiber, 1 mg sodium. Daily Value: 189% vit. C, 27% folate, 18% thiamine, 10% calcium, 21% potassium.*

# Spring Salad

*Subtly sweet jicama adds a crisp bite to this salad.*

- 1/3  cup Citrus Base (see recipe, page 43)
- 2    tablespoons salad oil
- 1    tablespoon sugar
- 1/4  teaspoon ground cinnamon
- 4    cups torn fresh spinach
- 3    cups torn leaf lettuce
- 1    cup Florida Grapefruit and/or Florida Orange Sections, seeded
- 1    cup peeled jicama cut into thin, bite-size strips
- 1    cup sliced strawberries

For dressing, in a screw-top jar combine Citrus Base, oil, sugar, and cinnamon. Cover and shake well to blend.

In a salad bowl toss together spinach and lettuce. Drizzle with *half* of the dressing mixture; toss together to mix. To serve, divide the greens mixture among 6 salad plates. Arrange citrus sections, jicama, and strawberries on the greens; drizzle with remaining dressing. Makes 6 side-dish servings.

**Per serving:** *125 cal., 2 g pro., 15 g carbo., 7 g total fat (1 g sat. fat), 0 mg cholesterol, 3 g dietary fiber, 105 mg sodium. Daily Value: 97% vit. C, 39% vit. A, 64% folate, 11% riboflavin, 10% calcium, 13% iron, 24% potassium.*

# Citrus and Papaya Salad

*For an easy meal, serve this sunny salad with ham or turkey and steamed broccoli.*

| | |
|---|---|
| 1 | teaspoon finely shredded Florida Orange Peel |
| ¼ | cup Florida Orange Juice |
| ¼ | cup salad oil |
| 1½ | teaspoons poppy seed |
| 1 | papaya |
| 2 | Florida Red Grapefruit |
| 1 | head Belgian endive |
| | Boston or Bibb lettuce leaves |
| ⅓ | cup sliced almonds (optional) |
| | Red-tip Belgian endive leaves (optional) |

For dressing, in a screw-top jar combine orange peel, orange juice, salad oil, and poppy seed. Cover and shake well. Chill for at least 1 hour.

Seed, peel, and slice papaya lengthwise. Peel, section, and seed the grapefruit. Slice the Belgian endive crosswise into 8 pieces.

Line 4 salad plates with the Boston or Bibb lettuce leaves. Arrange the papaya slices, grapefruit sections, and sliced Belgian endive atop the lettuce leaves. Sprinkle with almonds, if desired. Shake dressing well; pour over each salad. Garnish each serving with the red-tip Belgian endive leaves, if desired. Makes 4 side-dish servings.

**Per serving:** *204 cal., 2 g pro., 20 g carbo., 14 g total fat (1 g sat. fat), 0 mg cholesterol, 4 g dietary fiber, 4 mg sodium. Daily Value: 174% vit. C, 33% folate, 10% thiamine, 23% potassium.*

# Orange and Beet Spinach Salad

*Celebrate the advent of spring with this colorful, crisp salad.*

| | |
|---|---|
| 2 | small fresh beets or one 8-ounce can beets, chilled, drained, and cut into julienne strips |
| 6 | cups torn fresh spinach, leaf lettuce, and/or romaine |
| 3 | Florida Oranges, peeled, thinly sliced, and seeded |
| ½ | of a medium cucumber, thinly sliced |
| ½ | cup Orange Dressing (see recipe, page 43) |

To cook fresh beets, if using, remove tops and wash beets. In a medium saucepan cook whole, unpeeled beets, covered, in a small amount of lightly salted boiling water about 35 minutes or until tender. Transfer beets to a small bowl. Cover and chill until ready to serve. Peel beets and cut into julienne strips.

To serve, divide greens among 6 salad plates. Top each serving with some of the beet strips, orange slices, and cucumber slices. Drizzle with Orange Dressing. Makes 6 side-dish servings.

**Per serving:** *145 cal., 3 g pro., 15 g carbo., 10 g total fat (1 g sat. fat), 0 mg cholesterol, 4 g dietary fiber, 133 mg sodium. Daily Value: 95% vit. C, 50% vit. A, 77% folate, 14% thiamine, 12% riboflavin, 12% calcium, 12% iron, 27% potassium.*

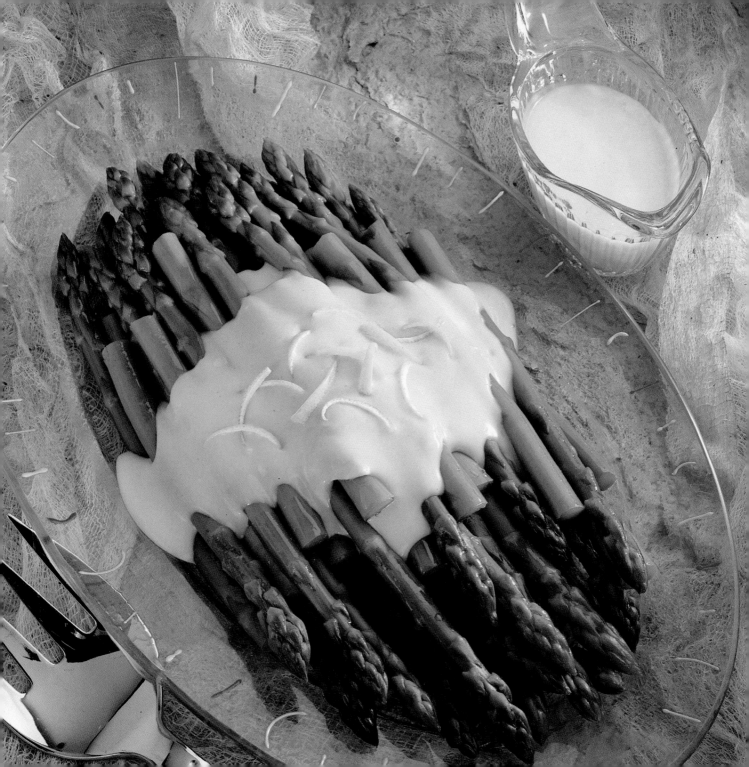

# Asparagus with Zesty Orange Sauce

*What could be easier? Just stir four ingredients together for this luscious sauce and heat for a minute or two. Next time, serve the sauce with green beans or potatoes.*

| | |
|---|---|
| 2 | pounds asparagus spears or 1½ pounds broccoli |
| ⅓ | cup frozen Florida Orange Juice *Concentrate*, thawed |
| ⅓ | cup fat-free mayonnaise dressing |
| 1 | teaspoon Dijon-style mustard |
| | Dash pepper |
| | Thin strips of Florida Orange Peel |

Wash asparagus spears; scrape off scales, if desired. Break off woody bases and discard. Or, wash and remove outer leaves of broccoli and tough parts of stalks; cut lengthwise into spears.

Place asparagus or broccoli in a steamer basket over simmering water. Cover and steam for 7 to 9 minutes for asparagus or 8 to 12 minutes for broccoli or until vegetables are crisp-tender. Carefully remove steamer basket and reserve 2 tablespoons of the steaming liquid.

For sauce, in a small saucepan whisk together the thawed orange juice concentrate, mayonnaise dressing, mustard, and pepper until smooth. Stir in 1 to 2 tablespoons of the reserved liquid to make sauce the desired consistency. Cook and stir over low heat for 1 to 2 minutes or until heated through. *Do not boil.*

To serve, arrange asparagus or broccoli on a serving platter; spoon sauce over spears. Garnish with strips of orange peel. Makes 8 servings.

**Per serving:** *49 cal., 3 g pro., 12 g carbo., 0 g total fat (0 g sat. fat), 0 mg cholesterol, 2 g dietary fiber, 104 mg sodium. Daily Value: 50% vit. C, 90% folate, 20% thiamine, 13% riboflavin, 12% niacin, 19% potassium.*

Add a little sunshine to lunch boxes and brown-bag meals by tucking in a Florida Orange, Tangerine, or Tangelo. The sweet, juicy fruit will provide energy to complete the day, plus valuable vitamins and fiber.

When packing lunches for children, cut the oranges into fun "smiles" or "points" (see directions, page 78), so little ones won't need to remove the peel. Tangerines, the zipper-skin fruit, are so easy to peel that kids can peel the fruit themselves.

← **Asparagus with Zesty Orange Sauce**

## Skillet Sweet Potatoes

*Give traditional candied sweet potatoes a new twist with snappy orange flavor and a speedy skillet method.*

| | |
|---|---|
| 1 | pound sweet potatoes, peeled and sliced ½ inch thick |
| ½ | teaspoon finely shredded Florida Orange Peel |
| ½ | cup Florida Orange Juice |
| 2 | tablespoons brown sugar or molasses |
| 1 | tablespoon margarine or butter |
| ½ | teaspoon pumpkin pie spice |
| ¼ | teaspoon salt |

Place sweet potatoes in a 12-inch skillet; cover with boiling water and cook, covered, about 10 minutes or until potatoes are tender. Drain well.

Meanwhile, for sauce, in a small mixing bowl combine orange peel, orange juice, brown sugar or molasses, margarine or butter, pumpkin pie spice, and salt. Pour over the cooked potatoes in the skillet. Cook and stir until bubbly. Boil gently, uncovered, about 5 minutes or until potatoes are glazed, spooning sauce over potatoes occasionally. Makes 4 servings.

**Per serving:** *177 cal., 2 g pro., 35 g carbo., 3 g total fat (1 g sat. fat), 0 mg cholesterol, 4 g dietary fiber, 174 mg sodium. Daily Value: 39% vit. C, 247% vit. A, 12% folate, 14% riboflavin, 14% potassium.*

## Squash with Orange Sauce

*A range of cinnamon is suggested so you can adjust the spiciness to suit your family.*

| | |
|---|---|
| 4 | small acorn squash, halved and seeds removed, or 3 pounds Hubbard squash, cut into 8 pieces and seeds removed |
| ¾ | cup frozen Florida Orange Juice *Concentrate,* thawed |
| 2 | tablespoons margarine or butter |
| 2 | tablespoons brown sugar |
| ¼ | to ½ teaspoon ground cinnamon |
| ⅛ | teaspoon ground nutmeg |
| ¼ | cup slivered almonds, toasted |
| 8 | Florida Tangerine or Orange Slices |

Place squash pieces, cut side up, in a large baking pan. Cover and bake in a 350° oven for 1 hour.

For sauce, in a small saucepan combine thawed orange juice concentrate, margarine or butter, brown sugar, cinnamon, and nutmeg. Heat until margarine is melted. Remove from heat.

Pour sauce in or over squash shells and return squash to oven. Bake, uncovered, about 35 minutes more or until squash is tender. Sprinkle with almonds. Garnish with tangerine or orange slices. Makes 8 servings.

**Per serving:** *150 cal., 2 g pro., 26 g carbo., 5 g total fat (1 g sat. fat), 0 mg cholesterol, 5 g dietary fiber, 30 mg sodium. Daily Value: 50% vit. C, 12% vit. A, 31% folate, 23% thiamine, 29% potassium.*

## Wild Rice Pilaf

*Orange juice concentrate replaces part of the liquid in the rice mix, giving the pilaf a tantalizing punch.*

| | |
|---|---|
| ¾ | cup frozen Florida Orange Juice **Concentrate**, thawed |
| | **Reduced-sodium chicken broth (about 2¾ cups)** |
| ½ | cup chopped onion |
| ¼ | teaspoon pepper |
| 2 | 6-ounce packages long grain and wild rice mix |
| ¼ | cup snipped parsley |

In a measuring cup combine thawed orange juice concentrate and enough chicken broth for the mixture to equal the amount of liquid called for on the combined packages of the rice mix.

In a large saucepan combine the juice mixture, onion, and pepper. Bring mixture to boiling. Stir in rice and accompanying seasoning mix. Return to boiling; reduce heat. Cover and simmer about 25 minutes or until rice is tender and liquid is absorbed. Remove from heat; stir in parsley. Serves 8 to 10.

**Per serving:** *205 cal., 6 g pro., 45 g carbo., 1 g total fat (0 g sat. fat), 0 mg cholesterol, 1 g dietary fiber, 974 mg sodium. Daily Value: 38% vit. C, 21% folate, 19% thiamine, 19% niacin, 18% iron, 12% potassium.*

## Orange Rice

*Make this easy side dish to round out a broiled fish, chicken, or ham dinner.*

| | |
|---|---|
| 2 | cups water |
| 1 | tablespoon frozen Florida Orange Juice **Concentrate**, thawed |
| ¼ | teaspoon salt |
| 1 | cup long grain rice |
| ¼ | cup thinly sliced green onions |

In a medium saucepan combine water, thawed orange juice concentrate, and salt. Bring to boiling; add rice. Return to boiling; reduce heat. Cover and simmer for 15 minutes. Remove from heat. Stir in green onions. Cover and let stand 5 minutes. Makes 6 servings.

**Per serving:** *119 cal., 2 g pro., 26 g carbo., 0 g total fat (0 g sat. fat), 0 mg cholesterol, 0 g dietary fiber, 94 mg sodium. Daily Value: 19% thiamine, 10% niacin.*

Here's a timesaving tip: When a recipe calls for shredded orange or grapefruit peel, shred some extra peel and stash it in the freezer for another use. (You'll get about 4 teaspoons shredded peel from a medium orange or a small grapefruit.) Place extra peel in a small freezer bag, seal, label, and date the package.

# Citrus Dressings

**Dress up a salad with one of these delectable citrus-sparked salad dressings. You'll turn an ordinary salad into a unique combination of flavors.**

## Grapefruit-Mint Dressing

*Replacing vinegar with grapefruit juice adds a fruity tang, while corn syrup adds sweetness and body to this salad dressing.*

| | |
|---|---|
| ½ | cup Florida Grapefruit Juice |
| ¼ | cup salad oil |
| 2 | tablespoons light corn syrup |
| 1 | tablespoon snipped fresh mint or ½ teaspoon dried mint, crushed |

In a screw-top jar combine grapefruit juice, oil, corn syrup, and mint. Cover and shake well to mix. Chill in the refrigerator at least 1 hour before serving. Store in the refrigerator up to 2 weeks. Shake well before serving. Serve over fruit salad or meat or poultry salads. Makes about 1 cup.

**Per tablespoon:** *40 cal., 0 g pro., 3 g carbo., 3 g total fat (0 g sat. fat), 0 mg cholesterol, 0 g dietary fiber, 3 mg sodium. Daily Value: none.*

## Oil-Free Dressing

*At last, a delicious homemade dressing that's fat free! Honey and pectin give the dressing fullness that oil usually supplies.*

| | |
|---|---|
| ¼ | teaspoon finely shredded Florida Orange Peel |
| ⅓ | cup Florida Orange Juice |
| 1 | tablespoon powdered fruit pectin* |
| 1 | tablespoon honey |
| ¼ | teaspoon poppy seed |

In a small nonmetallic bowl stir together orange peel, orange juice, pectin, honey, and poppy seed. Cover and chill in the refrigerator for several hours or overnight before serving. Store in the refrigerator up to 3 days. Serve over fruit salad. Makes about ½ cup.

**\*Note:** Look for pectin with canning supplies in the supermarket.

**Per tablespoon:** *18 cal., 0 g pro., 5 g carbo., 0 g total fat (0 g sat. fat), 0 mg cholesterol, 0 g dietary fiber, 0 mg sodium. Daily Value: none.*

## Citrus Base

¾ cup frozen Florida Orange Juice
    Concentrate, thawed
¼ cup Florida Grapefruit Juice
¼ cup salad oil
¼ cup white wine Worcestershire sauce
2 tablespoons sugar
1½ teaspoons dried basil, crushed
¾ teaspoon garlic salt
¾ teaspoon onion powder
½ teaspoon celery seed
¼ teaspoon pepper
    Several dashes bottled hot pepper sauce

In a large screw-top jar combine the thawed orange juice concentrate, grapefruit juice, salad oil, white wine Worcestershire sauce, sugar, basil, garlic salt, onion powder, celery seed, pepper, and hot pepper sauce. Cover and shake well to mix. Use at once or store in the refrigerator up to 2 weeks. Use in salad dressings (see recipe below or Spring Salad recipe, page 35) or as a marinade for fish or beef (see recipes, pages 13 and 17). Or, brush the mixture on vegetables during grilling or broiling. Makes 1½ cups.

**Per tablespoon:** *39 cal., 0 g pro., 5 g carbo., 2 g total fat (0 g sat. fat), 0 mg cholesterol, 0 g dietary fiber, 81 mg sodium. Daily Value: 19% vit. C.*

### Easy Citrus Salad Dressing:

In a screw-top jar combine ⅓ cup *Citrus Base* and 2 tablespoons *salad oil*. Cover and shake well to mix. Drizzle over tossed salads. Makes about ½ cup.

**Per tablespoon:** *56 cal., 0 g pro., 3 g carbo., 5 g total fat (0 g sat. fat), 0 mg cholesterol, 0 g dietary fiber, 54 mg sodium. Daily Value: 12% vit. C.*

## Orange Dressing

*If you plan to use all of this zippy dressing right away, make it with either olive oil or salad oil. If you don't need the entire half cup of dressing, divide the recipe or use salad oil, as olive oil solidifies when stored in the refrigerator.*

¼ cup olive oil or salad oil
1 teaspoon finely shredded Florida Orange Peel
¼ cup Florida Orange Juice
1 tablespoon Dijon-style mustard
⅛ teaspoon pepper

In a screw-top jar combine olive or salad oil, orange peel, orange juice, Dijon-style mustard, and pepper. Cover and shake well to mix. Serve with fruit, vegetable, or seafood salads. Makes about ½ cup.

**Per tablespoon:** *60 cal., 0 g pro., 1 g carbo., 6 g total fat (0 g sat. fat), 0 mg cholesterol, 0 g dietary fiber, 52 mg sodium. Daily Value: none.*

# Bountiful Breads

**W**ake up to a healthful breakfast or brunch of fresh-baked bread, filled through and through with delightful Florida Citrus flavor. Using convenience products, you can whip up morning delights, such as Orange-Pecan Ring, pictured at left, and Stuffed French Toast. Or, for unexpected guests or gift-giving, make ahead and freeze the Orange-Date Loaves and Orange-Chocolate Muffins.

For an added treat, try the selection of citrus-sparked spreads and toppings, perfect for any bread or toast.

← **Orange-Pecan Ring**
(see recipe, page 46)

# Orange-Pecan Ring

*Orange juice takes the place of brown sugar flavor in this yummy version of sticky rolls. Pictured on pages 44–45.*

| | |
|---|---|
| 2 | **tablespoons water** |
| 2 | **teaspoons cornstarch** |
| ¾ | **cup frozen Florida Orange Juice** *Concentrate*, **thawed** |
| ¼ | **cup sugar** |
| 2 | **tablespoons margarine or butter** |
| 2 | **tablespoons light corn syrup** |
| ½ | **cup chopped pecans** |
| 1 | **16-ounce package hot roll mix** |
| 2 | **tablespoons sugar** |
| 1 | **tablespoon finely shredded Florida Orange Peel** |
| ¼ | **cup sugar** |
| ¾ | **teaspoon ground cinnamon** |

In a small saucepan combine the water and cornstarch; stir in the thawed orange juice concentrate, ¼ cup sugar, margarine or butter, and corn syrup. Cook and stir until mixture is thickened and bubbly. Stir in pecans. Set aside.

Prepare roll mix according to package directions adding the 2 tablespoons sugar and the orange peel to the mix. Divide dough into 32 pieces. Form each piece of dough into a ball. Pour *half* of the orange mixture into the bottom of a lightly greased 10-inch fluted tube pan. Place *half* of the dough balls atop the orange mixture.

In a small mixing bowl combine the other ¼ cup sugar and the cinnamon. Sprinkle *half* of the sugar mixture over the dough balls in the pan. Repeat layers of remaining orange mixture, dough balls, and sugar mixture. Cover and let rise in a warm place until nearly double (about 30 minutes).

Bake in a 350° oven for 30 to 35 minutes or until golden brown. Let stand on a rack for 2 to 3 minutes. Loosen sides and invert onto a serving plate. If any topping remains in pan, spread atop the ring. Cool about 20 minutes; serve warm. Makes 10 servings.

**Per serving:** *318 cal., 6 g pro., 59 g carbo., 7 g total fat (1 g sat. fat), 0 mg cholesterol, 1 g dietary fiber, 338 mg sodium. Daily Value: 34% vit. C, 20% folate, 41% thiamine, 25% riboflavin, 20% niacin.*

Shredded peel from a Florida Orange adds lots of flavor to a variety of foods, from breads to desserts. To shred the peel of an orange, wash the fruit with tap water, then dry thoroughly with a paper towel. Working over a piece of waxed paper, push the orange across a shredding surface with small holes to make long, narrow strips of peel. Turn the orange before each stroke so you are scraping off just the orange-colored zest. Or, pull a zesting tool from the top to the bottom of the orange, turning the fruit with each stroke.

# Cinnamon-Orange Pinwheels

*Serve these fancy rolls for lunch with a salad or for midmorning treats.*

| | |
|---|---|
| 1 | 16-ounce package hot roll mix |
| 2 | tablespoons sugar |
| 1 | tablespoon finely shredded Florida Orange Peel |
| 1 | cup Florida Orange Juice |
| 2 | tablespoons margarine or butter |
| 1 | slightly beaten egg |
| 2 | tablespoons margarine or butter, melted |
| 16 | pecan or walnut halves |
| 1 | beaten egg white |
| 2 | tablespoons sugar |
| ½ | teaspoon ground cinnamon |

In a large bowl combine the hot roll mix, contents of the accompanying yeast packet, the 2 tablespoons sugar, and orange peel.

In a small saucepan combine the orange juice and the 2 tablespoons margarine or butter. Heat until warm (120° to 130°) and margarine or butter is almost melted. Add to flour mixture along with the egg, stirring until dough pulls away from sides of bowl.

Turn the dough out onto a lightly floured surface. With floured hands shape the dough into a ball. Knead 5 minutes or until smooth. Cover and let rest for 10 minutes.

On a floured surface roll dough into a 16-inch square. If needed, cover the dough and let rest 5 minutes to make rolling easier. Brush dough with the melted margarine or butter. Cut dough into sixteen 4-inch squares. Transfer the dough squares onto 2 greased baking sheets. Shape into pinwheels; top with nuts as directed at right.

Lightly brush the pinwheels with egg white; sprinkle with the remaining 2 tablespoons sugar and the cinnamon. Cover pinwheels with a towel. Let rise until double (about 15 minutes). Press nuts slightly to keep points in place. Bake in a 375° oven about 15 minutes or until golden. Serve warm. Makes 16 rolls.

**Per serving:** *181 cal., 4 g pro., 27 g carbo., 7 g total fat (1 g sat. fat), 13 mg cholesterol, 0 g dietary fiber, 227 mg sodium. Daily Value: 10% vit. C, 22% thiamine, 17% riboflavin, 12% niacin.*

To shape the pinwheels, start by cutting from the corner of each square toward the center, stopping ½ inch from the center. Fold every other point of dough to the center and overlap slightly in the center. Press a nut-half in the center to hold the points down.

# Orange-Date Loaves

*Serve with Fluffy Orange Butter, if desired.*

- 4  cups all-purpose flour
- 3/4  cup sugar
- 2  teaspoons baking powder
- 2  teaspoons finely shredded Florida Orange Peel
- 1/2  teaspoon baking soda
- 1/2  teaspoon salt
- 2  beaten eggs
- 3/4  cup frozen Florida Orange Juice *Concentrate*, thawed
- 1/3  cup cooking oil
- 1  8-ounce package chopped pitted dates
- 1/2  cup chopped pecans or walnuts

In a large mixing bowl stir together flour, sugar, baking powder, orange peel, baking soda, and salt. In another mixing bowl stir together eggs, *½ cup* of the thawed orange juice concentrate, the oil, and 1½ cups *water*. Add to flour mixture. Stir by hand just until combined. Fold in dates and nuts.

Divide mixture evenly between two greased 8x4x2-inch loaf pans. Bake in a 350° oven for 50 to 55 minutes or until a toothpick inserted near the centers comes out clean. (Or, divide mixture evenly among four 5½x3x2-inch loaf pans and bake for 40 to 45 minutes or until loaves test done.) Cool in pans for 10 minutes; remove from pans. Generously brush tops and sides of loaves with remaining orange juice concentrate. Cool thoroughly on wire racks. Wrap and store overnight before slicing. Makes 2 loaves (16 servings each).

**Per serving:** *140 cal., 2 g pro., 24 g carbo., 4 g total fat (0 g sat. fat), 13 mg cholesterol, 1 g dietary fiber, 71 mg sodium. Daily Value: 9% vit. C, 16% thiamine.*

# Orange-Chocolate Muffins

*Orange juice concentrate replaces part of the milk in the muffins, giving them extra flavor.*

- 3  cups all-purpose flour
- 2/3  cup sugar
- 2  teaspoons baking powder
- 1/4  teaspoon baking soda
- 2  beaten eggs
- 1  cup milk
- 1/2  cup cooking oil
- 1/3  cup frozen Florida Orange Juice *Concentrate*, thawed
- 2  teaspoons finely shredded Florida Orange Peel
- 1  cup miniature semisweet chocolate pieces Frozen Florida Orange Juice *Concentrate*, thawed (optional)

Grease twenty-four 2½-inch muffin cups or line the cups with paper bake cups. Set the muffin pans aside.

In a large mixing bowl stir together flour, sugar, baking powder, baking soda, and ½ teaspoon *salt*. Make a well in the center. In another mixing bowl stir together eggs, milk, oil, thawed orange juice concentrate, and orange peel. Add all at once to flour mixture. Stir just until moistened (batter should be lumpy). Stir in chocolate pieces.

Fill prepared muffin cups ⅔ full. Bake in a 400° oven for 18 to 20 minutes or until golden. Remove from pans; serve warm. If desired, brush muffin tops with a little orange juice concentrate. Makes 24 muffins.

**Per serving:** *170 cal., 3 g pro., 24 g carbo., 7 g total fat (2 g sat. fat), 19 mg cholesterol, 1 g dietary fiber, 91 mg sodium. Daily Value: 7% vit. C, 14% thiamine, 10% riboflavin.*

← **Orange-Chocolate Muffins, Orange-Date Loaves, and Fluffy Orange Butter (see recipe, page 52)**

# Stuffed French Toast with Orange-Blueberry Sauce

*If you're watching your cholesterol and fat, prepare this French toast with refrigerated or frozen egg product instead of whole eggs.*

|     |     |
| --- | --- |
| 1 | 16-ounce loaf French bread |
| 1 | cup light ricotta cheese |
| 2 | tablespoons chopped toasted walnuts |
| ½ | teaspoon finely shredded Florida Orange Peel |
| 2 | 2½-ounce packages very thinly sliced fully cooked ham |
|   | Nonstick spray coating |
| 4 | beaten eggs or 1 cup refrigerated or frozen egg product, thawed |
| ½ | cup Florida Orange Juice |
| ½ | cup milk |
| 2 | Florida Oranges |
|   | Florida Orange Juice |
| ½ | cup sugar |
| 2 | tablespoons cornstarch |
| ½ | cup fresh blueberries |
| 1 | tablespoon margarine or butter |
|   | Powdered sugar |

Cut French bread into ten to twelve 1-inch-thick slices. Cut a pocket in each bread slice by making a cut in the center of the top crust of each slice, cutting through the bread almost to the bottom crust.

For stuffing, stir together the ricotta cheese, walnuts, and orange peel. Fill each pocket with some of the cheese mixture and some of the ham, dividing evenly among pockets.

Spray a baking sheet with nonstick coating. In a shallow bowl stir together the eggs or egg product, the ½ cup orange juice, and milk. Dip each stuffed bread slice into the egg mixture, coating both sides while being careful not to squeeze out the filling.

Place dipped toast on the prepared baking sheet. Bake in a 450° oven for 8 minutes. Turn the slices over and bake about 10 minutes more.

Meanwhile, for sauce, peel, section, and seed the oranges over a bowl to catch juices. Add enough additional orange juice to the reserved juices to make 1½ cups.

In a medium saucepan combine the sugar and cornstarch. Stir in the 1½ cups orange juice. Cook and stir over medium heat until thickened and bubbly. Cook and stir 2 minutes more. Stir in the orange sections, blueberries, and margarine or butter.

To serve, sift powdered sugar over stuffed toast. Pass warm sauce with the stuffed toast. Makes 5 or 6 servings.

**Per serving:** *611 cal., 28 g pro., 95 g carbo., 14 g total fat (4 g sat. fat), 197 mg cholesterol, 5 g dietary fiber, 1,034 mg sodium. Daily Value: 90% vit. C, 17% vit. A, 45% folate, 88% thiamine, 67% riboflavin, 51% niacin, 28% calcium, 25% iron, 31% potassium.*

# Nutty Orange Pancakes

*Using orange juice instead of milk in the batter gives these pancakes a special twist.*

| | |
|---|---|
| 1 | cup all-purpose flour |
| 1 | tablespoon sugar |
| 2 | teaspoons baking powder |
| ½ | teaspoon baking soda |
| ½ | teaspoon ground cinnamon |
| ¼ | teaspoon salt |
| 1 | beaten egg |
| 1 | cup Florida Orange Juice |
| 2 | tablespoons cooking oil |
| ¼ | cup finely chopped nuts |
| | Orange Sauce (see recipe, at right) |
| | or maple syrup (optional) |

In a medium mixing bowl stir together flour, sugar, baking powder, baking soda, cinnamon, and salt. In another mixing bowl combine egg, orange juice, and cooking oil. Add all at once to flour mixture. Stir mixture just until combined (batter should be slightly lumpy). Stir in the nuts.

Pour about ¼ *cup* of the batter onto a hot, lightly greased griddle or heavy skillet for each standard-size pancake or about *1 tablespoon* batter for each dollar-size pancake.

Cook until pancakes are golden brown, turning to cook second sides when pancakes have bubbly surfaces and slightly dry edges. Serve with Orange Sauce or maple syrup, if desired. Makes 4 servings (8 to 10 standard-size or 36 dollar-size pancakes).

**Per serving:** *284 cal., 6 g pro., 36 g carbo., 14 g fat (1 g sat. fat), 53 mg cholesterol, 2 g dietary fiber, 412 mg sodium. Daily Value: 35% vit. C, 4% vit. A, 17% folate, 37% thiamine, 20% riboflavin, 16% niacin, 14% calcium, 15% iron.*

# Orange Sauce

*For a taste treat, ladle this smooth sauce over pancakes, gingerbread, or frozen yogurt.*

| | |
|---|---|
| ¼ | cup sugar |
| 1 | tablespoon cornstarch |
| ¼ | teaspoon finely shredded Florida Orange Peel |
| ¾ | cup Florida Orange Juice |
| 2 | teaspoons margarine or butter |

In a small saucepan combine sugar, cornstarch, and orange peel. Stir in orange juice. Cook and stir over medium heat until thickened and bubbly. Cook and stir 2 minutes more. Remove from heat; stir in margarine or butter. Serve warm. Makes 4 servings.

**Per serving:** *94 cal., 0 g pro., 19 g carbo., 2 g total fat (0 g sat. fat), 0 mg cholesterol, 0 g dietary fiber, 17 mg sodium. Daily Value: 26% vit. C.*

How much fruit or juice do you get from a medium orange? One orange yields ⅓ cup sections or ¼ to ⅓ cup juice. To get the most juice from each orange, let it stand at room temperature about 30 minutes, then roll the orange on the counter under the palm of your hand a few times before juicing.

# Spreads and Toppings

**Turn pancakes, waffles, muffins, French toast, or plain toast into tempting treats with one of these flavorful toppings.**

## Fluffy Orange Butter

*The few minutes you spend whipping up this top-notch topping will be well worth the effort.*

| | |
|---|---|
| ½ | cup margarine or butter, softened |
| 1½ | cups sifted powdered sugar |
| ¼ | cup frozen Florida Orange Juice Concentrate, thawed |

In a small mixing bowl beat margarine or butter with an electric mixer on medium speed for 30 seconds. Then, beat in the powdered sugar.

Gradually beat in the thawed orange juice concentrate. Serve at once or cover and chill to store. Makes 1½ cups.

**Per tablespoon:** *63 cal., 0 g pro., 7 g carbo., 4 g total fat (1 g sat. fat), 0 mg cholesterol, 0 g dietary fiber, 32 mg sodium. Daily Value: none.*

## Cinnamon-Orange Topper

*Enjoy this tasty, spicy citrus spread on pancakes or French toast.*

| | |
|---|---|
| ½ | of an 8-ounce package reduced-fat cream cheese (Neufchâtel), softened |
| ¼ | cup margarine or butter, softened |
| 1 | cup sifted powdered sugar |
| ¼ | to ½ teaspoon ground cinnamon |
| ¼ | cup frozen Florida Orange Juice Concentrate, thawed |

In a mixing bowl beat cream cheese and margarine or butter with an electric mixer on medium speed until combined. Beat in powdered sugar and cinnamon.

Gradually beat in the thawed orange juice concentrate. Serve at once or cover and chill to store. Makes 1 cup.

**Per tablespoon:** *74 cal., 1 g pro., 8 g carbo., 4 g total fat (1 g sat. fat), 5 mg cholesterol, 0 g dietary fiber, 53 mg sodium. Daily Value: 10% vit. C.*

# Orange Marmalade

4     medium Florida Oranges
1     medium lemon
1½    cups water
⅛     teaspoon baking soda
5     cups sugar
½     of a 6-ounce package liquid fruit pectin
      (1 foil pouch)*

Score the peels of the oranges and lemon into 4 lengthwise sections. Remove peels from fruits; scrape off white portions. Cut the peels into very thin strips. In a saucepan combine orange and lemon peels, water, and baking soda. Bring to boiling; reduce heat. Cover and simmer for 20 minutes. *Do not drain.*

Remove membranes from the peeled oranges and lemon. Section the fruits over a bowl to catch juices. Discard seeds. Add fruits and reserved juices to peel mixture. Return to boiling; reduce heat. Cover and simmer for 10 minutes. Measure *3 cups.*

In an 8- or 10-quart kettle combine the 3 cups fruit mixture and sugar. Bring to a full rolling boil. Quickly stir in pectin; return to a full boil. Boil and stir, uncovered, for 1 minute. Remove from heat; skim off foam. Ladle at once into hot, sterilized half-pint jars, leaving a ¼-inch headspace. Adjust lids. Process in a boiling-water canner for 15 minutes. (Marmalade may take up to 2 weeks to set.) Makes about 6 half-pints.

*Note: Look for pectin with canning supplies in the supermarket.

**Per tablespoon:** *44 cal., 0 g pro., 11 g carbo., 0 g total fat (0 g sat. fat), 0 mg cholesterol, 0 g dietary fiber, 1 mg sodium. Daily Value: none.*

# Orange Syrup

*This luscious warm sauce isn't just for breakfast—try it over frozen vanilla yogurt, too.*

½     cup margarine or butter
½     cup sugar
⅓     cup frozen Florida Orange Juice
      *Concentrate,* thawed

In a small saucepan combine margarine or butter, sugar, and thawed orange juice concentrate. Cook and stir over low heat until margarine is melted. *Do not boil.* Remove from heat and cool for 10 minutes. Using a rotary beater, beat until slightly thickened. Serve warm. Makes ¾ cup.

**Per tablespoon:** *113 cal., 0 g pro., 11 g carbo., 8 g total fat (1 g sat. fat), 0 mg cholesterol, 0 g dietary fiber, 65 mg sodium. Daily Value: 18% vit. C.*

# All-Occasion Beverages

Add a new twist to your refreshments with the fresh taste of Florida Orange and Grapefruit Juices. Whether you're serving after-school snacks or a formal reception, in this chapter you'll find delicious beverages to delight the crowd. Orange-Grapefruit Fizz, Orange Fizz, and Grapefruit Fizz, pictured at left, will be a hit with adults and kids.

These beverages are a snap to make and brimming with vitamin C, so fill the glasses and toast your health!

← Orange-Grapefruit Fizz, Orange Fizz, and Grapefruit Fizz
(see recipes, page 56)

## Orange Fizz

*Here's a vitamin-packed, easy alternative to bottled soft drinks—a delicious beverage kids and adults will love. Pictured on pages 54–55.*

> ¾   **cup frozen Florida Orange Juice** *Concentrate,* **thawed**
> 2¼   **cups carbonated water or tonic water, chilled**
>      **Ice cubes**
>      **Florida Grapefruit Slices, quartered (optional)**

Pour the thawed orange juice concentrate into a pitcher. Gently stir in the chilled carbonated water or tonic water. To serve, pour over ice cubes in glasses. If desired, garnish with quartered grapefruit slices. Serve at once. Makes 4 (6-ounce) servings.

**Per serving:** *73 cal., 1 g pro., 18 g carbo., 0 g total fat (0 g sat. fat), 0 mg cholesterol, 0 g dietary fiber, 28 mg sodium. Daily Value: 98% vit. C, 37% folate, 12% thiamine, 14% potassium.*

## Grapefruit Fizz

*For a colorful, two-tone drink (as pictured on pages 54–55), add a little grenadine syrup to each glass and leave it unstirred.*

> ¾   **cup frozen Florida Grapefruit Juice** *Concentrate,* **thawed**
> 1   **1-liter bottle carbonated water or tonic water, chilled**
>      **Grenadine syrup (optional)**
>      **Florida Orange Slices, halved (optional)**
>      **Fresh mint sprigs (optional)**

Pour thawed grapefruit juice concentrate into a pitcher. Gently stir in the chilled carbonated water. If desired, add grenadine syrup to each glass and garnish with halved orange slices and mint sprigs. Serve at once. Makes about 6 (6-ounce) servings.

**Per serving:** *41 cal., 1 g pro., 10 g carbo., 0 g total fat (0 g sat. fat), 0 mg cholesterol, 0 g dietary fiber, 36 mg sodium. Daily Value: 56% vit. C.*

## Orange-Grapefruit Fizz

*Pictured on pages 54–55.*

> ¾   **cup frozen Florida Orange Juice** *Concentrate,* **thawed**
> ¾   **cup frozen Florida Grapefruit Juice** *Concentrate,* **thawed**
> 1   **1-liter bottle carbonated water or tonic water, chilled**
>      **Ice cubes**

In a pitcher combine thawed orange and grapefruit juice concentrates. Gently stir in the carbonated water. To serve, pour over ice cubes in glasses. Serve at once. Makes about 7 (6-ounce) servings.

**Per serving:** *74 cal., 1 g pro., 18 g carbo., 0 g total fat (0 g sat. fat), 0 mg cholesterol, 0 g dietary fiber, 32 mg sodium. Daily Value: 104% vit. C, 23% folate, 10% thiamine, 14% potassium.*

# Fruit Frosties

*Whip up this nutritious orange juice drink for an after-school treat, or serve it to grown-ups instead of frozen daiquiris.*

1½   cups cold water
1    10-ounce package frozen
     strawberries, thawed
¾    cup frozen Florida Orange Juice
     *Concentrate,* thawed
1    ripe banana, cut up
1    to 2 cups ice cubes
     **Whole fresh strawberries (optional)**
1    **Florida Orange, sliced and halved
     (optional)**

In a blender container or food processor bowl combine water, thawed strawberries, orange juice concentrate, and banana pieces. Cover and blend or process until smooth. While the blender or processor is running, add the ice cubes through the hole in the lid, blending or processing until smooth and slushy.

To serve, pour into glasses. If desired, garnish with whole strawberries and halved orange slices. Serve at once. Makes 6 (8-ounce) servings.

**Per serving:** *108 cal., 1 g pro., 28 g carbo., 0 g total fat (0 g sat. fat), 0 mg cholesterol, 1 g dietary fiber, 2 mg sodium. Daily Value: 101% vit. C, 30% folate, 16% potassium.*

# Orangeade

2¼   cups cold water
¾    cup frozen Florida Orange Juice
     *Concentrate,* thawed
¼    cup lemon juice (about 1 large lemon)
2    tablespoons sugar
     Ice cubes

In a pitcher stir together the thawed orange juice concentrate and water. Add lemon juice and sugar, stirring until sugar is dissolved. To serve, pour over ice cubes in glasses. Makes 4 (7-ounce) servings.

**Per serving:** *96 cal., 1 g pro., 24 g carbo., 0 g total fat (0 g sat. fat), 0 mg cholesterol, 0 g dietary fiber, 1 mg sodium. Daily Value: 109% vit. C, 38% folate, 12% thiamine, 15% potassium.*

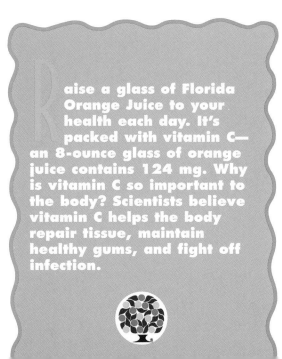

Raise a glass of Florida Orange Juice to your health each day. It's packed with vitamin C—an 8-ounce glass of orange juice contains 124 mg. Why is vitamin C so important to the body? Scientists believe vitamin C helps the body repair tissue, maintain healthy gums, and fight off infection.

# Orange-Spice Tea

*Trying to cut down on caffeine? Enjoy this hot drink as a morning energizer or as an afternoon pick-me-up.*

| | |
|---|---|
| 2 | cups water |
| 3 | inches stick cinnamon, broken |
| 6 | whole cloves |
| 2 | tea bags |
| 1 | cup Florida Orange Juice |
| 1 | tablespoon brown sugar |
| | Florida Orange Points (optional) (see directions, page 78) |

In a medium saucepan combine water, cinnamon, and cloves. Bring to boiling; remove from heat. Add tea bags and let stand for 5 minutes. Remove tea bags.

Stir in the orange juice and brown sugar. Heat through. To serve, pour mixture through a wire strainer into mugs. If desired, garnish with orange points. Makes 4 (6-ounce) servings.

**Per serving:** *38 cal., 0 g pro., 9 g carbo., 0 g total fat (0 g sat. fat), 0 mg cholesterol, 0 g dietary fiber, 5 mg sodium. Daily Value: 35% vit. C, 14% folate.*

# Orange Cider

*This delightful warmer takes about 10 minutes to prepare.*

| | |
|---|---|
| 2 | cups Florida Orange Juice |
| ⅓ | cup frozen apple juice *concentrate*, thawed (½ of a 6-ounce can) |
| 2 | tablespoons orange liqueur or nonalcoholic orange liqueur |

In a saucepan combine orange juice, apple juice concentrate, and ½ cup *water*. Cook over medium heat 8 to 10 minutes or until hot, stirring occasionally. Stir in liqueur. To serve, pour into mugs. Makes 5 (5-ounce) servings.

**Microwave directions:** In a 4-cup microwave-safe measure combine orange juice, apple juice concentrate. and ½ cup *water*. Micro-cook, uncovered, on 100% power (high) for 6 to 7 minutes or until hot, stirring every 2 minutes. Stir in liqueur. To serve, pour into mugs.

**Per serving:** *97 cal., 1 g pro., 20 g carbo., 0 g total fat (0 g sat. fat), 0 mg cholesterol, 0 g dietary fiber, 6 mg sodium. Daily Value: 55% vit. C, 17% folate, 14% potassium.*

When you have a portion of a can of frozen Florida Orange or Grapefruit Juice Concentrate left over from a recipe, prepare ready-to-serve juice following these measurements:

- to ⅓ cup concentrate, add 1 cup water
- to ½ cup concentrate, add 1½ cups water
- to ¾ cup concentrate, add 2¼ cups water
- to 1¼ cups concentrate, add 3¾ cups water.

## Iced Tea with a Twist

*Once you've tasted this tangy citrus-flavored tea, it's sure to become a favorite for meals and refreshments.*

| | |
|---|---|
| 4 | cups cold strong tea* |
| 1 | cup Florida Orange Juice |
| ½ | cup Florida Grapefruit Juice |
| ¼ | to ⅓ cup sugar |
| | Ice cubes |
| | Strips of orange and grapefruit peel (optional) |

In a large pitcher combine tea, orange juice, and grapefruit juice. Stir in desired amount of sugar to taste.

To serve, pour over ice cubes in glasses. If desired, tie a strip of orange peel and a strip of grapefruit peel into a knot; use as a garnish. Makes about 8 (6-ounce) servings.

**Note:** To brew the strong tea, use 4½ cups water and 10 individual tea bags.

**Per serving:** *45 cal., 0 g pro., 11 g carbo., 0 g total fat (0 g sat. fat), 0 mg cholesterol, 0 g dietary fiber, 4 mg sodium. Daily Value: 36% vit. C, 10% folate.*

## Sunshine Slush

*The subtle spiced flavor makes this a great nonalcoholic drink for entertaining.*

| | |
|---|---|
| 1½ | cups water |
| ½ | cup sugar |
| 2 | inches stick cinnamon |
| ¾ | cup frozen Florida Orange Juice *Concentrate*, thawed |
| ¾ | cup frozen Florida Grapefruit Juice *Concentrate*, thawed |
| 1 | 1-liter bottle carbonated water, chilled |

In a small saucepan combine the water, sugar, and stick cinnamon. Bring to boiling; reduce heat. Cover and simmer for 5 minutes. Remove and discard the cinnamon stick. Cool.

In a bowl or pitcher combine the sugar mixture and thawed concentrates. Stir until combined. Pour mixture into a 9x5x3- or 11x7x1½-inch baking pan. Freeze for several hours or until firm.

To serve, let mixture stand at room temperature about 20 minutes. To form a slush, scrape a large spoon across the frozen mixture. Divide mixture into 8 glasses. Slowly pour the carbonated water down the side of each glass. Stir gently to mix. Serve with swizzle sticks or straws. Serve at once. Makes 8 (7-ounce) servings.

**Per serving:** *113 cal., 1 g pro., 28 g carbo., 0 g total fat (0 g sat. fat), 0 mg cholesterol, 0 g dietary fiber, 28 mg sodium. Daily Value: 91% vit. C, 20% folate, 12% potassium.*

# Nectarine-Orange Sunrise

*For interesting red and gold swirls, use a swizzle stick or straw to stir the drink very lightly in a circular motion after pouring the orange-nectarine mixture over the grenadine.*

| | |
|---|---|
| 3 | nectarines |
| ¾ | cup frozen Florida Orange Juice *Concentrate*, thawed |
| ⅔ | cup tequila |
| | Crushed ice |
| ½ | cup grenadine syrup |
| | Fresh mint sprigs |
| 1 | Florida Orange, sliced and halved |

Halve, pit, and coarsely chop the nectarines. In a blender container combine the chopped nectarines, thawed orange juice concentrate, and tequila. Cover and blend until smooth. Gradually add crushed ice, blending until mixture is slushy and measures 5 cups.

To serve, place *1 tablespoon* of the grenadine syrup in *each* of 8 stemmed glasses. Add orange-nectarine mixture. To garnish, top each with a mint sprig and hang a halved orange slice on the side of each glass. Serve at once. Makes 8 (5-ounce) servings.

**Per serving:** *117 cal., 1 g pro., 18 g carbo., 0 g total fat (0 g sat. fat), 0 mg cholesterol, 2 g dietary fiber, 1 mg sodium. Daily Value: 70% vit. C, 22% folate, 16% potassium.*

# Citrus Eye-Opener

*Kick off a brunch or a leisurely weekend breakfast with tall glasses of this zippy drink.*

| | |
|---|---|
| 1 | 12-ounce can frozen Florida Orange Juice *Concentrate*, thawed |
| 1 | 6-ounce can frozen lemonade concentrate, thawed |
| 1½ | cups cold water |
| 1 | 1-liter bottle carbonated water, chilled |
| | Ice cubes |
| 1 | Florida Orange, sliced and halved (optional) |

In a large pitcher combine the thawed concentrates and the cold water.

Just before serving, slowly add carbonated water. Stir gently to mix. To serve, pour over ice cubes in glasses. If desired, garnish the glasses with halved orange slices. Serve at once. Makes 8 (7- to 8-ounce) servings.

**Per serving:** *106 cal., 1 g pro., 26 g carbo., 0 g total fat (0 g sat. fat), 0 mg cholesterol, 0 g dietary fiber, 28 mg sodium. Daily Value: 104% vit. C, 38% folate, 12% thiamine, 15% potassium.*

# Daiquiri Punch

*If the occasion calls for a nonalcoholic punch, just omit the peach schnapps.*

| | |
|---|---|
| 1 | 12-ounce can frozen Florida Orange Juice *Concentrate*, thawed |
| 1 | 12-ounce can frozen pink lemonade *concentrate*, thawed |
| 2 | 6-ounce cans frozen strawberry daiquiri mix *concentrate*, thawed |
| 2¼ | cups cold water |
| 2 | cups peach or apricot nectar |
| ⅓ | cup peach schnapps |
| 4 | 12-ounce cans lemon-lime carbonated beverage, chilled |
| | Ice cubes or ice ring |
| | Strawberries (optional) |

In a punch bowl or large bowl combine thawed orange juice concentrate, lemonade concentrate, and daiquiri mix concentrate. Stir in water, peach or apricot nectar, and schnapps. Cover and chill until serving time.

To serve, slowly add carbonated beverage and ice cubes or ice ring. Float strawberries atop punch, if desired. Serve at once. Makes about 20 (6-ounce) servings.

**Per serving:** *158 cal., 1 g pro., 37 g carbo., 0 g total fat (0 g sat. fat), 0 mg cholesterol, 0 g dietary fiber, 11 mg sodium. Daily Value: 46% vit. C, 16% folate.*

# Citrus Bubbly

*Celebrate an anniversary, promotion, or any special occasion with this champagne drink.*

| | |
|---|---|
| 2 | cups cold water |
| ¾ | cup frozen Florida Orange Juice *Concentrate*, thawed |
| 2 | tablespoons sugar |
| 1 | 750-milliliter bottle champagne, chilled |
| | Ice cubes (optional) |

In a pitcher combine water, thawed orange juice concentrate, and sugar. Stir until thoroughly mixed.

To serve, slowly pour in chilled champagne. Stir gently to mix. Serve in glasses or punch cups. If desired, serve over ice. Serve at once. Makes 12 (4-ounce) servings.

**Per serving:** *79 cal., 0 g pro., 9 g carbo., 0 g total fat (0 g sat. fat), 0 mg cholesterol, 0 g dietary fiber, 4 mg sodium. Daily Value: 33% vit. C, 12% folate.*

← **Daiquiri Punch**

## Citrus Spritzer

*Offer this enticing beverage with appetizers or when relaxing after a busy day.*

| | |
|---|---|
| 2 | cups Florida Orange Juice |
| ½ | cup dry white wine |
| | Ice cubes |
| 1 | cup carbonated water, chilled |
| 1 | Florida Orange, cut into wedges (optional) |

In a pitcher or serving bowl stir together orange juice and wine. Add ice cubes.

Slowly add the carbonated water. Serve in wine glasses or punch cups. If desired, garnish with orange wedges. Serve at once. Makes 4 (7-ounce) servings.

**Per serving:** *75 cal., 1 g pro., 13 g carbo., 0 g total fat (0 g sat. fat), 0 mg cholesterol, 0 g dietary fiber, 15 mg sodium. Daily Value: 103% vit. C, 21% folate, 11% thiamine, 13% potassium.*

## Citrus Mimosa

*This dazzling blend of fruit flavors will delight brunch or weekend guests.*

| | |
|---|---|
| 1 | cup prepared strawberry daiquiri mix |
| ¾ | cup frozen Florida Orange Juice *Concentrate*, thawed |
| ¾ | cup cold water |
| ⅓ | cup Florida Grapefruit Juice |
| ⅓ | cup frozen lemonade *concentrate*, thawed |
| 3 | tablespoons frozen limeade *concentrate*, thawed |
| | Ice cubes |
| | Chilled champagne |
| 1 | Florida Orange, thinly sliced and halved (optional) |

In a pitcher or bowl combine prepared daiquiri mix, thawed orange juice concentrate, water, grapefruit juice, thawed lemonade concentrate, and limeade concentrate. Stir until well mixed. Cover and chill until serving time.

To serve, pour the chilled juice mixture into 8 ice-filled glasses, filling each glass half full. Pour an equal amount of chilled champagne into each glass. Garnish with orange slice halves, if desired. Serve at once. Makes 8 (6-ounce) servings.

**Per serving:** *158 cal., 1 g pro., 24 g carbo., 0 g total fat (0 g sat. fat), 0 mg cholesterol, 0 g dietary fiber, 9 mg sodium. Daily Value: 60% vit. C, 20% folate, 12% potassium.*

# Festive Grapefruit Punch

*For a baby shower, reception, or graduation celebration, add
grenadine syrup to give the punch a soft pink color.*

|   |   |
|---|---|
| 1 | cup cold water |
| ¾ | cup frozen Florida Grapefruit Juice *Concentrate*, thawed |
| 1 | 6-ounce can frozen pineapple juice *concentrate*, thawed |
| 3 | tablespoons honey |
| 2 | tablespoons grenadine syrup (optional) |
| 1 | 1-liter bottle ginger ale, chilled |
|   | Ice ring or ice cubes |

In a punch bowl or large pitcher combine cold water,
thawed grapefruit juice and pineapple juice concentrates, and honey. If desired, add grenadine syrup.
Stir until combined.

To serve, slowly pour chilled ginger ale down the side of
the bowl or pitcher. Stir gently to mix. Add ice ring or
serve over ice in chilled glasses or punch cups. Serve at
once. Makes about 18 (4-ounce) servings.

**Per serving:** *61 cal., 0 g pro., 15 g carbo., 0 g total fat
(0 g sat. fat), 0 mg cholesterol, 0 g dietary fiber, 5 mg
sodium. Daily Value: 25% vit. C.*

Brighten up your punch bowl and keep the beverage cold at the same time with a festive ice ring. To prepare, select a ring mold that fits into the punch bowl. Fill the mold half full with water and freeze until firm (about 4 hours). Cut 3 Florida Orange Wheels or Slices in half and arrange the half-slices on top of the frozen ice layer. If desired, top each orange slice with a cluster of 3 whole cranberries and clean lemon or orange leaves. Add enough water to cover fruit. Freeze until firm. Unmold the ice ring and place it in the punch bowl. Consider making several ice rings so you can replace them as they melt.

# Light Desserts

Satisfy your sweet tooth with this selection of tempting yet light desserts. Tangy Florida Citrus takes the place of high-fat ingredients without sacrificing an ounce of flavor. Treat yourself to such sensations as Frozen Orange Swirl Pie, pictured at left, and light-as-a-cloud Orange Angel Cake. Also, look for the section on easy garnishes to add glamour to every course of the meal.

←Frozen Orange Swirl Pie
(see recipe, page 68)

# Frozen Orange Swirl Pie

*A snappy gingersnap crust complements the flavor of the ice-cream pie. Pictured on pages 66–67.*

| | |
|---|---|
| ¼ | **cup sugar** |
| 4 | **teaspoons cornstarch** |
| ¾ | **cup frozen Florida Orange Juice** *Concentrate, thawed* |
| ⅓ | **cup water** |
| 2 | **tablespoons margarine or butter, cut up** |
| 1 | **tablespoon finely shredded Florida Orange Peel** |
| 1¼ | **cups finely crushed gingersnaps** |
| ⅓ | **cup margarine or butter, melted** |
| 6 | **cups vanilla frozen yogurt or low-fat or light vanilla ice cream** |
| | **Fresh mint sprigs (optional)** |

For sauce, in a medium saucepan combine sugar and cornstarch; stir in thawed orange juice concentrate and water. Cook and stir over medium heat until thickened and bubbly. Cook and stir for 2 minutes more. Remove from heat; stir in the 2 tablespoons margarine or butter and orange peel. Cover and cool completely.

For crust, in a medium bowl combine crushed gingersnaps and the ⅓ cup melted margarine. Toss to mix well. Spread mixture evenly into a 9-inch pie plate. Press onto bottom and sides to form a firm, even crust. Chill about 1 hour or until firm.

Place *4 cups* of the frozen yogurt or ice cream into a chilled bowl. Use a wooden spoon to stir the yogurt to soften slightly. Spoon the softened yogurt into the crumb crust. Drizzle *half* of the cool orange sauce over the yogurt. Swirl sauce into the yogurt with a knife or narrow metal spatula.

Remove remaining 2 cups of frozen yogurt from the freezer. Make small scoops of yogurt with an ice-cream dipper and arrange over pie. (Or, use a spoon to make small scoops of yogurt.) Do not smooth over top evenly. Drizzle the remaining orange sauce over all. Cover and freeze at least 8 hours before serving. If desired, garnish with mint sprigs. Makes 8 servings.

**Per serving:** *388 cal., 7 g pro., 58 g carbo., 15 g total fat (4 g sat. fat), 12 mg cholesterol, 0 g dietary fiber, 264 mg sodium. Daily Value: 35% vit. C, 21% vit. A, 25% folate, 10% thiamine, 21% riboflavin, 27% calcium, 24% potassium.*

# Country Compote

*No fat, no cholesterol, but loaded with flavor—this fresh fruit temptation is sure to please your crowd.*

| 2 | cups fruity white wine |
|---|---|
| ½ | cup raisins |
| ¼ | cup honey |
| 2 | teaspoons finely shredded lemon peel |
| 4 | Florida Oranges, peeled, sectioned, and seeded |
| 2 | cups sliced strawberries or 2 medium pears |
| 1 | pomegranate (optional) |

Place wine and raisins in a small container; cover and soak raisins overnight.

To prepare the compote, drain raisins, reserving wine. Set raisins aside. In a medium saucepan combine reserved wine, honey, and lemon peel. Bring to boiling; reduce heat. Simmer, uncovered, for 2 minutes. Set aside to cool.

Cut orange sections in half. Add oranges and raisins to the wine mixture; stir gently. Transfer to a large serving bowl. Cover and chill at least 4 hours or up to 24 hours.

To serve, if using pears, cut into bite-size pieces. Top the orange mixture with strawberries or pears and, if desired, sprinkle with pomegranate seeds. Makes 6 servings.

**Per serving:** *196 cal., 2 g pro., 37 g carbo., 0 g total fat (0 g sat. fat), 0 mg cholesterol, 4 g dietary fiber, 7 mg sodium. Daily Value: 132% vit. C, 21% folate, 11% thiamine, 21% potassium.*

all on Florida Citrus Fruit for a healthful, easy ending for a meal. Simply pass a platter of Florida Grapefruit or Orange Sections. Or, for a special touch, arrange sliced oranges in dessert dishes and drizzle with honey or a mixture of honey and orange liqueur.

You'll be serving a refreshing, light treat, rich in vitamins and fiber, with little or no fat, cholesterol, or sodium. So indulge in the healthful sweetness of Florida Citrus Fruit.

# Orange-Berry Tart

*For a tantalizing twist, add a teaspoon of finely shredded Florida Orange Peel to the pastry mixture before adding the water.*

|       | Pastry for Single-Crust Pie (see recipe at right) |
|-------|---------------------------------------------------|
| 1     | 8-ounce package reduced-fat cream cheese (Neufchâtel), softened |
| ¼     | cup sugar                                         |
| 1     | teaspoon finely shredded Florida Orange Peel (set aside) |
| 1     | tablespoon Florida Orange Juice                   |
| ⅔     | cup Florida Orange Juice                          |
| 1     | tablespoon sugar                                  |
| 2     | teaspoons cornstarch                              |
| 2     | Florida Oranges, peeled, sectioned, and seeded    |
| 1     | pint strawberries, hulled and halved              |
|       | Thin strips of Florida Orange Peel (optional)     |
|       | Thin strips of lime peel (optional)               |

Prepare Pastry for Single-Crust Pie. On a lightly floured surface, flatten the ball of dough with hands. Roll dough from center to the edges forming a circle about 13 inches in diameter. Ease pastry into an 11-inch tart pan with removable bottom, being careful not to stretch the pastry. Trim even with edge of pan. Prick bottom and sides of the pastry generously with the tines of a fork. Bake in a 450° oven for 10 to 12 minutes or until golden. Cool pastry on a wire rack.

For filling, in a medium mixing bowl combine reduced-fat cream cheese, the ¼ cup sugar, and the 1 tablespoon orange juice. Beat with an electric mixer on high speed until light and fluffy. Stir in the 1 teaspoon orange peel. Spread filling in baked tart shell.

For orange glaze, in a small saucepan combine the ⅔ cup orange juice, the 1 tablespoon sugar, and cornstarch. Cook and stir over medium heat until mixture is thickened and bubbly. Cook and stir for 2 minutes more. Remove from heat. Cool completely.

Arrange orange sections then strawberry halves atop cheese filling. Spoon orange glaze over all. Sprinkle with thin strips of orange peel and lime peel, if desired. Cover and chill up to 6 hours. Remove sides of pan from tart and place tart on serving plate. Makes 10 servings.

**Pastry for Single-Crust Pie:** In a medium mixing bowl stir together 1¼ cups *all-purpose flour* and ¼ teaspoon *salt*. Cut in ¼ cup *shortening* until mixture resembles fine crumbs. Using 4 to 5 tablespoons *cold water*, sprinkle *1 tablespoon* of the water at a time over part of the mixture; gently toss with a fork. Push moistened dough to side of bowl. Repeat until all dough is moistened. Form dough into a ball.

**Per serving:** *214 cal., 5 g pro., 27 g carbo., 10 g total fat (5 g sat. fat), 16 mg cholesterol, 2 g dietary fiber, 146 mg sodium. Daily Value: 56% vit. C, 13% folate, 18% thiamine, 11% riboflavin.*

← **Orange-Berry Tart**

## Oranges with Gingersnaps and Dried Cherries

*The kids will have fun helping prepare this easy dessert for a weeknight supper.*

| | |
|---|---|
| 4 | medium Florida Oranges |
| | Florida Orange Juice |
| 1 | tablespoon honey |
| 1 | teaspoon cornstarch |
| ⅓ | cup dried cherries or mixed dried fruit bits |
| 2 | gingersnap cookies or 4 vanilla wafers, coarsely crumbled |

Working over a bowl to catch juices, peel, section, and seed oranges. Add enough additional orange juice to reserved juices to equal ½ cup juice total. Place orange sections on paper towels to drain.

For cherry sauce, in a small saucepan combine orange juice, honey, and cornstarch. Add dried cherries. Cook and stir over medium heat until thickened and bubbly. Cook and stir for 2 minutes more.

To serve, arrange orange sections on individual dessert plates. Spoon warm cherry sauce over orange sections. Top with the crumbled cookies. Makes 4 servings.

**Per serving:**
*140 cal., 2 g pro., 34 g carbo., 1 g total fat (0 g sat. fat), 0 mg cholesterol, 3 g dietary fiber, 21 mg sodium. Daily Value: 133% vit. C, 26% folate, 14% thiamine, 15% potassium.*

Fiber plays an important role in the diet. Dietary fiber aids in digestion and elimination. In addition, diets low in fat and rich in fruits and vegetables containing fiber may reduce the risk of some types of cancer. Citrus fruits are a natural source of dietary fiber. In fact, an orange or half grapefruit contains more fiber than any of the other top-20 most popular fruits.

# Orange Soufflé

Nonstick spray coating
2   egg yolks
1   teaspoon finely shredded Florida Orange
    Peel (set aside)
1   cup Florida Orange Juice
½   cup nonfat dry milk powder
6   tablespoons granulated sugar
2   tablespoons cornstarch
6   egg whites
½   teaspoon cream of tartar
    Powdered sugar

Spray a 2-quart rectangular baking dish with nonstick coating. Place yolks into a medium bowl. Set dish and yolks aside.

In a small saucepan combine orange juice, milk powder, *2 tablespoons* of the sugar, and the cornstarch. Cook and stir until thick and bubbly. (Mixture may appear curdled before it boils.) Cook and stir 2 minutes more. Stir about *half* of the mixture into yolks. Return all the mixture to saucepan. Cook and stir 2 minutes. Stir in peel. Remove from heat.

In a large mixing bowl beat egg whites and cream of tartar with an electric mixer on high speed until soft peaks form (tips curl). Gradually add remaining granulated sugar, *1 tablespoon* at a time, beating until stiff peaks form (tips stand straight).

Stir about *1 cup* of the beaten whites into yolk mixture. Gently fold yolk mixture into remaining beaten whites. Spoon into prepared dish. Bake in a 375° oven for 25 to 30 minutes or until puffed and golden. Sift powdered sugar over top. Serve immediately. Serves 8 to 10.

**Per serving:** *92 cal., 6 g pro., 13 g carbo., 2 g total fat (0 g sat. fat), 55 mg cholesterol, 0 g dietary fiber, 93 mg sodium. Daily Value: 18% vit. C, 13% folate, 18% riboflavin, 13% calcium, 12% potassium.*

# Citrus Crunch

*If you like warm fruit crisps, you'll love this lively citrus version.*

½    cup all-purpose flour
½    cup quick-cooking rolled oats
⅓    cup packed brown sugar
¼    cup margarine or butter
⅓    cup granulated sugar
4    teaspoons cornstarch
½    cup water
⅓    cup frozen Florida Orange Juice
     *Concentrate*, thawed
2½   cups Florida Orange Sections
1½   cups Florida Grapefruit Sections, cut up

In a mixing bowl combine flour, rolled oats, and brown sugar. Cut in the margarine or butter until mixture resembles coarse crumbs. Set mixture aside.

In a medium saucepan combine granulated sugar and cornstarch. Stir in the water and thawed orange juice concentrate. Cook and stir over medium heat until mixture is thickened and bubbly. Remove from heat. Gently stir in the orange and grapefruit sections. Pour mixture into a 2-quart square baking dish. Sprinkle with the oat mixture.

Bake in a 350° oven for 25 to 30 minutes or until topping is golden. Serve the dessert while warm. Makes 6 servings.

**Per serving:** *287 cal., 4 g pro., 52 g carbo., 8 g total fat (1 g sat. fat), 0 mg cholesterol, 4 g dietary fiber, 69 mg sodium. Daily Value: 88% vit. C, 15% vit. A, 31% folate, 26% thiamine, 10% riboflavin, 19% potassium.*

# Oranges in Caramel Syrup

*This masterful make-ahead dessert will provide a fine finale to a special dinner.*

½   cup sugar
1   cup warm water
2   tablespoons light rum or ¼ teaspoon
     rum flavoring
6   medium Florida Oranges
     Fresh red raspberries (optional)
     Fresh mint leaves (optional)

For syrup, place sugar in a heavy small skillet. Heat over medium-high heat until sugar begins to melt, shaking skillet occasionally to heat sugar evenly (do not stir). Reduce heat to low; cook until sugar is melted and golden (about 5 minutes more), stirring as necessary after sugar begins to melt and as mixture bubbles. Remove from heat.

Slowly pour in the warm water. Return to heat and cook over low heat until caramel dissolves. Slowly stir in rum or rum flavoring. Bring to boiling; reduce heat. Simmer, uncovered, for 5 minutes. Cool.

Using a vegetable peeler, remove the peel of *1 orange*. Cut peel into julienne strips and add to caramel syrup. Using a sharp paring knife, remove the peel and white membrane from all the oranges. Slice oranges, remove seeds, and place oranges in a shallow dish. Pour caramel syrup over oranges. Cover and chill for 2 to 24 hours.

To serve, place orange slices in dessert dishes. Spoon caramel syrup over oranges and, if desired, garnish with fresh raspberries and mint leaves. Makes 6 servings.

**Per serving:** *146 cal., 1 g pro., 34 g carbo. ,0 g total fat (0 g sat. fat), 0 mg cholesterol, 4 g dietary fiber, 0 mg sodium. Daily Value: 113% vit. C, 15% folate, 15% thiamine, 13% potassium.*

← **Oranges in Caramel Syrup**

When selecting oranges at the supermarket, remember the saying, "never judge a book by its cover." Even when Florida Oranges aren't bright orange on the outside, the fruit inside is deliciously ripe. The color of the peel (ranging from orange or yellow-orange to greenish yellow) is simply due to the tropical growing temperatures, which also make them so flavorful and juicy. Small blemishes on the skin, called wind scars, do not affect the quality of oranges either.

# Pink Grapefruit Sorbet

*Take a cue from fine restaurants and serve small scoops of this smooth sorbet as a refresher between courses. Or, serve it on a fruit salad or with sugar cookies for dessert.*

| | |
|---|---|
| 6 | **Florida Red Grapefruit** |
| 1 | **cup sugar** |
| 1 | **tablespoon lemon juice** |
| 1 | **tablespoon Campari (optional)** |

Using a vegetable peeler, remove the zest (colored part) from the peel of *1 grapefruit.* Coarsely chop the zest. In a food processor bowl or blender container combine chopped zest and sugar. Cover and process or blend until zest is very finely chopped.

Squeeze enough juice from the grapefruit to make *4 cups* juice; pour into a mixing bowl. Add zest mixture, lemon juice, and, if desired, Campari. Mix well.

Freeze the grapefruit mixture in a 2- or 4-quart ice cream freezer according to manufacturer's directions. Makes 1 quart or 8 (½-cup) servings.

**Per serving:** *153 cal., 1 g pro., 39 g carbo., 0 g total fat (0 g sat. fat), 0 mg cholesterol, 2 g dietary fiber, 0 mg sodium. Daily Value: 119% vit. C, 13% folate, 12% potassium.*

# Orange Sorbet

*A touch of shredded orange peel and orange juice concentrate give this frozen treat a pleasantly brisk flavor.*

| | |
|---|---|
| 2¾ | **cups water** |
| ¼ | **cup sugar** |
| ¾ | **cup frozen Florida Orange Juice *Concentrate*** |
| 1 | **teaspoon finely shredded Florida Orange Peel** |

In a small saucepan combine water and sugar. Cook and stir until sugar is dissolved. Cool to room temperature.

Add the frozen orange juice concentrate and the shredded orange peel. Stir until the concentrate is dissolved.

Freeze the mixture in a 1- or 2-quart ice cream freezer according to manufacturer's directions. Makes about 1 quart or 8 (½-cup) servings.

**Per serving:** *58 cal., 1 g pro., 14 g carbo., 0 g total fat (0 g sat. fat), 0 mg cholesterol, 0 g dietary fiber, 1 mg sodium. Daily Value: 49% vit. C, 18% folate.*

# Orange-Almond Frozen Yogurt

*Make your own frozen yogurt, either in the refrigerator freezer or ice cream freezer—whichever is most convenient.*

| | |
|---|---|
| 1 | envelope unflavored gelatin |
| ½ | cup cold water |
| 3 | 16-ounce cartons plain low-fat yogurt |
| ¾ | cup frozen Florida Orange Juice *Concentrate*, thawed |
| ½ | to ⅔ cup sugar |
| ¼ | teaspoon almond extract |
| ⅓ | cup chopped toasted almonds |

In a small saucepan stir gelatin into cold water; let stand for 5 minutes to soften. Cook and stir over low heat until gelatin is dissolved. Cool for 15 to 30 minutes.

In a large mixing bowl combine yogurt, thawed orange juice concentrate, sugar, and almond extract. Stir in gelatin mixture.

Pour into a nonmetallic freezer container. Freeze in the freezer section of the refrigerator until almost firm (about 6 hours).

Transfer mixture to a chilled large mixing bowl. Beat with an electric mixer until fluffy but not melted. Stir in almonds. Return mixture to freezer container. Freeze overnight or until firm.

Before serving, let yogurt stand several minutes at room temperature. Scoop into dishes or cones. Makes about 1¾ quarts or 12 to 14 (½-cup) servings.

**Ice-Cream Freezer Directions:** Prepare recipe as directed above, *except* after stirring in the gelatin, stir in the almonds. Freeze the mixture in a 4-quart ice cream freezer according to manufacturer's directions.

**Per serving:** *149 cal., 7 g pro., 23 g carbo., 4 g total fat (1 g sat. fat), 7 mg cholesterol, 1 g dietary fiber, 82 mg sodium. Daily Value: 34% vit. C, 21% folate, 10% thiamine, 23% riboflavin, 28% calcium, 19% potassium.*

I**f you're trying to improve your fitness or lose weight, exercise will give you a boost both physically and mentally. Start with something as simple as walking 15 minutes a day. After a few weeks, increase the time to 30 minutes a day. Walk briskly but be sure you don't become breathless. If you feel dizziness, pain, or light-headedness, stop. Consult your doctor before resuming your routine.**

**Use every opportunity to get some exercise; for example, take the stairs instead of the elevator. Make exercise and wise food choices part of your daily habits. Your increased energy and general health will reflect your efforts.**

# Picture-Perfect Garnishes

**Citrus fruits are a natural for garnishing desserts as well as main dishes, salads, and beverages. You'll find all the directions here.**

**← Citrus Sections:** Remove the peel from a Florida Orange or Grapefruit, either by cutting around the fruit in a spiral or cutting off peel in sections following the procedure described in the tip on page 5.

To section, work over a bowl to catch the juices. Cut between 1 fruit section and the membrane, as shown, cutting to the center of the fruit. Turn the knife and slide it up the other side of the section next to the membrane; repeat with remaining sections. Remove and discard seeds from the fruit.

**→ Citrus Twists:** Cut an unpeeled Florida Orange or lime into thin slices. Cut to the center of each slice, as shown, and twist the ends in opposite directions. Using 2 different fruit slices together gives a color contrast.

**Citrus Smiles:** Cut an unpeeled Florida Orange or Grapefruit in half crosswise. Cut each half diagonally into 3 or 4 wedges. Cut a slit to the center and hang over the lip of a glass as shown on page 88. Or eat out of hand.

**Orange Points:** To make points like those shown on page 58, cut an unpeeled Florida Orange in half lengthwise through the stem ends. Place a half cut side down and cut in half again through the stem ends. Holding 2 cut quarters side by side, slice crosswise, making orange points.

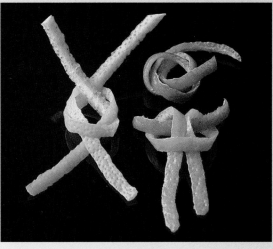

← Citrus Rose: Cut the peel from stem end of a Florida Orange or Grapefruit, forming a circular base (do not sever). Continue cutting a strip of peel about 3/4 to 1 inch wide in a spiral motion to opposite end, making one long, continuous strip and slicing thinly (do not cut into white membrane). Start coiling strip tightly, beginning at end opposite base. Coil strip onto base to form a rose. Garnish with mint leaves and small strips of peel, if desired.

→ Citrus Knots: Cut thin strips from Florida Orange or Grapefruit Peel or lime peel. Knot the citrus strips together, as shown at right.

## Candied Citrus Peel

*Dress up desserts with a sprinkle of these candied peels.*

|   |   |
|---|---|
| 2 | medium Florida Oranges, 4 medium Florida Tangerines, or 1 Florida Grapefruit |
| 1⅓ | cups sugar |
|   | Sugar (about ¼ cup) |

Cutting through the peels to the pulp, cut peels of the fruit into quarters. Use a spoon to loosen the peel from the pulp, leaving the white membrane attached to the peel. (Reserve pulp for another use.) Place fruit peel in a 2-quart nonmetallic bowl. Add enough cold water to cover. If necessary, place a plate in the bowl to keep peel submerged. Let stand overnight.

Drain the peel. Rinse with cold water. Place peel in a 2-quart saucepan. Cover with cold water. Bring to boiling; drain. Repeat boiling and draining peel 3 more times. Drain the peel, remove from pan, and cool thoroughly.

Cut the peel into ⅛- to ¼-inch-wide strips. In the same saucepan combine the 1⅓ cups sugar and ⅓ cup *water*.

Bring to boiling, stirring constantly to dissolve sugar. Add the peel. Return to boiling; reduce heat and cook over medium-low heat (mixture should boil at a moderate, steady rate over the entire surface), stirring occasionally, until peel is almost translucent. This should take 15 to 20 minutes. (*Do not overcook.*)

Using a slotted spoon, remove peel from syrup and place on wire racks set over waxed paper. Discard syrup. Cool until lukewarm. While peel is still slightly sticky, roll in additional sugar to coat. Dry on racks for 1 to 2 hours. Tightly cover and store in a cool, dry place up to 1 week or in the freezer up to 6 months. Makes about 2 cups peel.

# Orange Angel Cake

*Using orange juice concentrate in place of some of the water in the angel cake mix gives this cake a delicate orange flavor and color.*

| | |
|---|---|
| 1 | 15- or 16-ounce package angel cake mix |
| ¾ | cup frozen Florida Orange Juice *Concentrate,* thawed |
| 1 | 8-ounce container frozen light whipped dessert topping, thawed |
| ½ | cup plain low-fat yogurt Citrus Roses (optional) (see directions, page 79) |

Prepare angel cake as directed on package, *except* pour ⅓ *cup* of the thawed orange juice concentrate into a 2-cup measure; add enough *water* to the concentrate for the mixture to equal the amount of water called for in the package directions. Continue with package directions, baking the batter in an ungreased 10-inch tube pan according to package directions. Immediately invert cake (leave in pan); cool completely.

Loosen sides of cake from pan; remove cake from pan. For topping, in a medium bowl gently stir together the thawed topping and yogurt. Fold in remaining orange juice concentrate. Spread topping mixture over top and sides of cake. If desired, garnish with citrus roses made from grapefruit or orange peel. Store in the refrigerator. Makes 12 to 16 servings.

**Per serving:** *173 cal., 3 g pro., 33 g carbo., 3 g total fat (2 g sat. fat), 1 mg cholesterol, 0 g dietary fiber, 200 mg sodium. Daily Value: 27% vit. C, 14% folate.*

# Cranberry-Orange Cake

| | |
|---|---|
| | Nonstick spray coating |
| 1 | teaspoon all-purpose flour |
| 2 | cups all-purpose flour |
| 1 | cup granulated sugar |
| 1½ | teaspoons baking powder |
| ½ | teaspoon baking soda |
| 1 | egg |
| ¼ | cup cooking oil |
| 1 | tablespoon finely shredded Florida Orange Peel |
| ¾ | cup Florida Orange Juice |
| 1 | cup coarsely chopped cranberries |
| ¼ | cup finely chopped almonds, toasted |
| 1 | tablespoon all-purpose flour |
| 1 | tablespoon powdered sugar |

Spray an 8x8x2-inch baking pan with nonstick coating. Dust with the 1 teaspoon flour; set pan aside.

In a large mixing bowl combine the 2 cups flour, granulated sugar, baking powder, and baking soda. In another bowl combine egg, oil, orange peel, and orange juice; mix well. Add egg mixture to flour mixture, stirring just until combined. Toss together cranberries, almonds, and the 1 tablespoon flour. Stir into batter; pour into prepared pan.

Bake in a 350° oven about 40 minutes or until a toothpick inserted in the center comes out clean. Cool in pan on a wire rack for 10 minutes. Remove from pan; cool completely on rack. Sift powdered sugar over cooled cake. Makes 12 servings.

**Per serving:** *220 cal., 3 g pro., 37 g carbo., 7 g total fat (1 g sat. fat), 18 mg cholesterol, 1 g dietary fiber, 80 mg sodium. Daily Value: 11% vit. C, 19% thiamine, 13% riboflavin, 11% niacin.*

← **Orange Angel Cake**

# Grapefruit Chiffon Cake

*This airy, delicately flavored cake is worth every minute spent making it. Present it with pride for birthdays and celebrations.*

2¼   cups sifted cake flour or 2 cups sifted
       all-purpose flour
1½   cups sugar
1     tablespoon baking powder
¼     teaspoon salt
½     cup cooking oil
5     egg yolks
2     teaspoons finely shredded Florida
       Grapefruit Peel (set aside)
¾     cup Florida Grapefruit Juice
8     egg whites
½     teaspoon cream of tartar
       Grapefruit Icing
       Toasted sliced almonds

In a large bowl combine flour, sugar, baking powder, and salt. Add oil, egg yolks, and grapefruit juice. Beat with an electric mixer on low speed until combined. Beat on high speed for 5 minutes or until satin smooth. Stir in grapefruit peel.

Thoroughly wash beaters. In an extra-large bowl combine egg whites and cream of tartar. Beat on high speed until stiff peaks form (tips stand straight). Pour batter in a thin stream over beaten egg whites; fold in gently.

Pour into an ungreased 10-inch tube pan. Bake in a 325° oven for 65 to 70 minutes or until top springs back when lightly touched. Immediately invert cake (leave cake in pan); cool completely.

Loosen sides of cake from pan; remove cake from pan. Drizzle Grapefruit Icing over top of cake allowing some to drip down the sides. Sprinkle with almonds. Makes 12 servings.

**Grapefruit Icing:** In a medium bowl combine 1½ cups sifted *powdered sugar* and enough *Florida Grapefruit Juice* (1 to 2 tablespoons) to make of drizzling consistency. Makes about ½ cup.

**Per serving:** *339 cal., 5 g pro., 54 g carbo., 12 g total fat (1 g sat. fat), 89 mg cholesterol, 1 g dietary fiber, 161 mg sodium. Daily Value: 8% vit. C, 11% folate, 18% thiamine, 16% riboflavin, 10% niacin, 12% iron.*

# Gingerbread Torte

*If you're short on time, use the quick version.*

|       | Nonstick spray coating |
|-------|------------------------|
|       | All-purpose flour |
| 1½    | cups all-purpose flour |
| ¼     | cup sugar |
| 1½    | teaspoons pumpkin pie spice |
| ½     | teaspoon baking powder |
| ½     | teaspoon baking soda |
| ½     | cup molasses |
| ¾     | cup frozen Florida Orange Juice Concentrate, thawed (divided) |
| ⅓     | cup water |
| ¼     | cup margarine or butter, softened |
| 2     | egg whites |
| ½     | cup snipped pitted dates |
|       | Orange Filling |
|       | Orange Topping |

Spray an 8x8x2-inch baking pan with nonstick coating and dust lightly with all-purpose flour; set pan aside.

In a large bowl combine the 1½ cups flour, the sugar, pie spice, baking powder, and baking soda. Add molasses, ⅓ cup of the thawed orange juice concentrate, the water, margarine, and egg whites. Beat with an electric mixer on low to medium speed until combined. Beat on high speed 2 minutes more. Stir in dates. Pour into prepared pan.

Bake in a 350° oven about 35 minutes or until a toothpick inserted near the center comes out clean. Cool on a wire rack for 10 minutes. Remove from pan. Cool completely.

To assemble torte, split gingerbread layer horizontally. Fill with Orange Filling. Frost top and sides with Orange Topping. Cut into squares to serve. Store in the refrigerator. Makes 9 servings.

**Orange Filling:** In a small saucepan combine ½ cup *sugar* and 2 tablespoons *cornstarch*. Stir in ½ cup *water*, ¼ cup of the thawed *orange juice concentrate*, and 2 beaten *egg yolks*. Cook and stir over medium heat until thick and bubbly. Reduce heat. Cook and stir for 2 minutes. Stir in 1 tablespoon *margarine* until melted. Cover surface with plastic wrap. Cool without stirring.

**Orange Topping:** In a small bowl combine one 1.4-ounce envelope *whipped dessert topping mix* and ½ cup cold *milk*. Beat with an electric mixer on high speed about 4 minutes or until mixture forms stiff peaks (tips stand straight). Add remaining thawed *orange juice concentrate* (about 3 tablespoons). Beat on low speed just until mixed.

**Per serving:** *364 cal., 5 g pro., 66 g carbo., 10 g total fat (3 g sat. fat), 48 mg cholesterol, 2 g dietary fiber, 150 mg sodium. Daily Value: 49% vit. C, 15% vit. A, 26% folate, 25% thiamine, 16% riboflavin, 13% niacin, 11% calcium, 15% iron, 27% potassium.*

## Quick Gingerbread Torte

Spray an 8x8x2-inch baking pan with *nonstick spray coating;* lightly dust with *all-purpose flour.* Prepare one 14½-ounce package *gingerbread mix* according to package directions *except* use ⅓ cup frozen *Florida Orange Juice Concentrate,* thawed, combined with enough *water* for the mixture to equal the amount of liquid called for on the package directions. *Omit* the dates. Pour batter into prepared pan. Bake according to package directions. Cool on a wire rack 10 minutes. Remove from pan. Cool. Assemble, fill, and frost as in the Gingerbread Torte recipe.

**Per serving:** *282 cal., 4 g pro., 47 g carbo., 9 g total fat (4 g sat. fat), 64 mg cholesterol, 1 g dietary fiber, 235 mg sodium. Daily Value: 33% vit. C, 24% folate, 16% thiamine, 12% riboflavin, 12% iron, 14% potassium.*

# Orange-Chocolate Cake

*This moist cake is lower in fat because orange juice replaces part of the oil.*

|     | Nonstick spray coating |
|-----|------------------------|
|     | Unsweetened cocoa powder |
| 1   | package 2-layer-size devil's food cake mix |
| 1   | 8-ounce carton plain low-fat or nonfat yogurt |
| 2   | tablespoons finely shredded Florida Orange Peel (set aside) |
| ½   | cup Florida Orange Juice |
| ½   | cup water |
| 1   | egg |
| 2   | egg whites |
| 2   | tablespoons cooking oil |
| 1   | teaspoon ground cinnamon |
|     | Chocolate Icing |
|     | Orange Icing |
|     | Florida Orange Points (see directions, page 78) |

Spray a 10-inch fluted tube pan or a 13x9x2-inch baking pan with nonstick coating; dust with unsweetened cocoa powder. Set aside.

In a large mixing bowl combine cake mix, yogurt, orange juice, water, egg, egg whites, cooking oil, and cinnamon. Beat with an electric mixer on low speed for 4 minutes. Stir in orange peel. Pour into prepared pan.

Bake in a 350° oven for 40 to 50 minutes for tube pan or 35 to 40 minutes for a 13x9x2-inch baking pan or until a toothpick inserted near the center comes out clean. Cool in pan on a wire rack 10 minutes. Remove cake from tube pan or leave in 13x9x2-inch pan; cool completely. Drizzle icings over cake. Garnish with orange points. Makes 12 servings.

**Chocolate Icing:** In a small bowl combine ½ cup sifted *powdered sugar*, 1 tablespoon *unsweetened cocoa powder*, 2 teaspoons *Florida Orange Juice*, and ¼ teaspoon *vanilla*. Stir in enough additional *Florida Orange Juice* to make of drizzling consistency. Makes about 2 tablespoons.

**Orange Icing:** In a small bowl combine ½ cup sifted *powdered sugar*, 1 teaspoon *Florida Orange Juice*, and ¼ teaspoon *vanilla*. Stir in enough additional *Florida Orange Juice* to make of drizzling consistency. Makes about 2 tablespoons.

**Per serving:** *251 cal., 4 g pro., 44 g carbo., 8 g total fat (1 g sat. fat), 19 mg cholesterol, 0 g dietary fiber, 389 mg sodium. Daily Value: 8% vit. C, 10% riboflavin, 18% calcium.*

←**Orange-Chocolate Cake**

# Citrus Cookie Sandwiches

*Serve these dainty cookies with fresh fruit or frozen vanilla yogurt.*

| | |
|---|---|
| ½ | cup margarine or butter |
| 1 | 3-ounce package cream cheese, softened |
| 2 | cups all-purpose flour |
| 1 | cup sugar |
| 1 | egg |
| ½ | teaspoon baking powder |
| 2 | teaspoons finely shredded Florida Orange Peel (set aside) |
| ⅔ | cup Florida Orange Juice |
| ½ | teaspoon vanilla |
| ⅓ | cup sugar |
| 1 | tablespoon cornstarch |
| 1 | tablespoon margarine or butter |
| | Orange Glaze |

In a large mixing bowl beat the ½ cup margarine and cream cheese with an electric mixer on medium to high speed for 30 seconds. Add about *half* of the flour, the 1 cup sugar, egg, baking powder, *1 tablespoon* of the orange juice, and the vanilla. Beat until thoroughly combined. Beat or stir in the remaining flour until combined. Stir in *1 teaspoon* of the orange peel. Cover and chill 3 hours or until dough is easy to handle.

Meanwhile, for filling, in a small saucepan combine the ⅓ cup sugar and cornstarch. Add the remaining orange peel and the remaining orange juice. Cook and stir until mixture is thickened and bubbly. Cook and stir for 2 minutes more. Remove from heat. Stir in the 1 tablespoon margarine until melted. Cover; cool. Chill.

Divide the chilled dough in half. On a lightly floured surface, roll *half* of the dough at a time to ⅛-inch thickness. Cut with a scalloped, 2-inch round cookie cutter. Place 1 inch apart on ungreased cookie sheets.

Bake in a 375° oven about 8 minutes or until edges are lightly browned. Remove cookies from sheet and cool completely on a wire rack.

Up to 1 hour before serving, spread bottoms of *half* of the cookies with chilled orange filling. Top with remaining cookies. Brush lightly with Orange Glaze. Chill until serving time. Makes 40 sandwich cookies.

**Orange Glaze:** In a small mixing bowl stir together ½ cup sifted *powdered sugar* and enough *Florida Orange Juice* (2 to 3 teaspoons) to make of glaze consistency.

**Per serving:** *88 cal., 1 g pro., 13 g carbo., 4 g total fat (1 g sat. fat), 8 mg cholesterol, 0 g dietary fiber, 34 mg sodium. Daily Value: none.*

# Orange Brownies

*Take a tray of these heavenly brownies to the office to wow the gang.*

¼   **cup margarine or butter**
2    **ounces unsweetened chocolate, cut up**
¾   **cup sugar**
2    **eggs**
¼   **cup frozen Florida Orange Juice**
        **Concentrate, thawed**
1    **teaspoon finely shredded Florida**
        **Orange Peel**
1    **teaspoon vanilla**
¾   **cup all-purpose flour**
½   **cup chopped walnuts or pecans**
⅛   **teaspoon baking soda**
        **Orange-Fudge Frosting**

Grease an 8x8x2-inch baking pan; set aside. In a medium saucepan melt margarine or butter and chocolate over low heat, stirring constantly. Remove from heat. Cool 5 minutes. Add the sugar, eggs, thawed orange juice concentrate, shredded orange peel, and vanilla. Beat by hand just until combined.

Stir in flour, nuts, and baking soda until combined. Spread the batter in prepared baking pan.

Bake in a 350° oven for 20 minutes for a fudgy brownie. For a firmer brownie, bake 25 minutes. Cool in pan on a wire rack. Spread Orange-Fudge Frosting over cooled brownies. If desired, score frosting decoratively with tines of fork. Cut into bars. Makes 16 brownies.

**Orange-Fudge Frosting:** In a medium mixing bowl stir together 1½ cups sifted *powdered sugar* and 3 tablespoons *unsweetened cocoa powder*. Add 3 tablespoons softened *margarine* or *butter*, 1 tablespoon frozen *Florida Orange Juice Concentrate*, thawed, 1 tablespoon *boiling water*, and ½ teaspoon *vanilla*. Beat with an electric mixer on low speed until combined. Beat on medium speed for 1 minute more. Stir in ½ teaspoon finely shredded *Florida Orange Peel*.

**Per serving:** *202 cal., 3 g pro., 28 g carbo., 10 g total fat (2 g sat. fat), 27 mg cholesterol, 1 g dietary fiber, 58 mg sodium. Daily Value: 9% vit. C.*

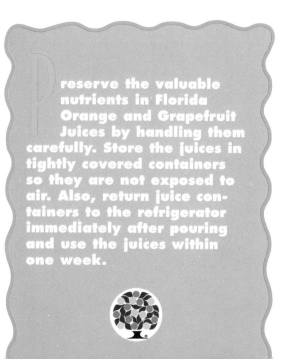

Preserve the valuable nutrients in Florida Orange and Grapefruit Juices by handling them carefully. Store the juices in tightly covered containers so they are not exposed to air. Also, return juice containers to the refrigerator immediately after pouring and use the juices within one week.

# Here's to Your Health

Antioxidants... Folate... Carotenoids... **Is your head swimming with nutrition terms and advice? Registered Dietitian Elaine Waldschmitt offers simple explanations and guidelines for healthful eating.**

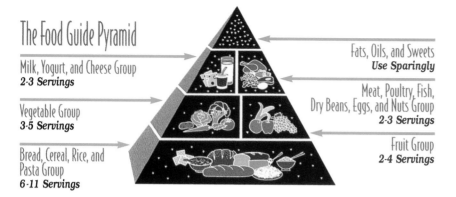

## The Food Guide Pyramid

**Fats, Oils, and Sweets**
*Use Sparingly*

**Milk, Yogurt, and Cheese Group**
*2-3 Servings*

**Meat, Poultry, Fish, Dry Beans, Eggs, and Nuts Group**
*2-3 Servings*

**Vegetable Group**
*3-5 Servings*

**Fruit Group**
*2-4 Servings*

**Bread, Cereal, Rice, and Pasta Group**
*6-11 Servings*

Tidal waves of new research are confirming what nutritionists have been saying all along: There is a strong connection between eating a balanced diet and staying healthy. The way we choose to eat—or choose not to eat—has life-long effects.

Despite the abundance of nutritional information, eating for health is not complicated. A person doesn't need a degree in nutrition to make sound nutritional choices. Recently, the U.S. Department of Agriculture released its Food Guide Pyramid, which is designed to help Americans develop variety, moderation, and proportionality in their diets. The pyramid symbol (shown above) visually emphasizes which foods need to be increased in the diet to enhance health and which foods should be limited. Fruits and vegetables are presented as separate groups, because each group provides distinct nutrients, and *both* vegetables *and* fruits should be included in the daily diet.

If Americans adopt the eating style the Food Guide Pyramid recommends, overall health and nutrition will be improved. The benefits of a healthful diet can be achieved from eating plenty of vegetables

and fruits, and yet these groups are the very ones most often neglected. Diet surveys report Americans consume only 9 percent of the recommended servings of fruits and vegetables. Most people get less than half of the folate and iron they need. Many people don't consume enough vitamin C, despite the fact that one 8-ounce glass of orange juice supplies the day's needs.

**The good news is that it's easy to improve your diet—simply increase the amount of fruits and vegetables you eat each day.**

An examination of almost 200 published scientific studies by the National Cancer Institute and the University of California at Berkeley demonstrated that people who ate the most fruits and vegetables had about half the cancer risk of people who ate fewer fruits and vegetables. Many scientists and nutritionists are convinced that a high consumption of fruits and vegetables can guard against heart disease and illnesses such as diabetes and gastrointestinal diseases.

Citrus fruits play a crucial role in nutritional wellness, strengthen our immunities, and help fight off diseases such as cancer and heart disease. Some nutrients found in citrus that are linked to disease prevention include:

• **Antioxidants:** The main antioxidants are vitamin C, beta carotene, and vitamin E. They strengthen the body's natural defenses against cell damage as well as play a

role in reducing atherosclerosis, the disease that leads to heart attacks and strokes. Citrus fruits are excellent sources of antioxidants.

• **Vitamin C:** This powerful antioxidant, abundant in citrus fruits, has many roles. It helps heal wounds, aids in the absorption of iron, contributes to collagen formation (collagen is necessary to hold cells together), and also may help reduce the risks of certain cancers. New research on vitamin C intake and heart disease shows that people who consume 300 mg or more of vitamin C daily have a 42 percent lower risk of heart disease than people who consume 50 mg or less.

• **Folate:** This vitamin is essential for the formation of all body cells. Folate also is important for healthy blood, because it helps in the formation of hemoglobin, which carries oxygen in the blood.

Research has linked women's deficient folate intake with the incidence of neural-tube defects (such as spina bifida and anencephaly) in their babies. The U.S. Food and Drug Administration advises that a woman can reduce the risk of having a child with neural-tube defects by consuming plenty of folate *prior* to pregnancy. Orange juice is an excellent dietary source of folate. Additional research documents diets deficient in folate, B12, and B6 may put individuals at risk for developing heart disease.

• **Carotenoids:** Nutritionists are just beginning to learn about these plant pigments that act as antioxidants and have been linked to cancer prevention. Good sources are deep-yellow or orange fruits and vegetables, such as red grapefruit and carrots.

• **Fiber:** Fiber is abundant in fresh and cooked fruits and vegetables, cereals, and grains. Fiber decreases the risk of colon cancer and other bowel diseases. Studies have linked high-fiber diets with the lowering of low-density lipoproteins, or "bad" cholesterol, a contributing factor in heart disease.

• **Fat and cholesterol:** Lowering total fat and cholesterol has long been a nutritional goal in America. The impact of high-fat diets on disease is clearly documented. Most fruits and vegetables are fat-free, and cholesterol is found only in foods of animal origin.

• **Natural sugar:** The average American diet is very high in refined sugar. Eating foods loaded with refined sugar, such as regular soft drinks and most desserts, requires the body to respond with bursts of chemicals to help stabilize the blood-sugar level. Eating fresh fruit provides natural sugar, which allows for a slower, more healthy release of body chemicals.

• **Weight control:** Almost every American has at one time or another attempted to limit his or her food intake to avoid gaining unwanted pounds or to lose a few that were already on board! The Food Pyramid guides a person through weight loss without sacrificing healthful eating.

**The more fruits and vegetables you eat, the less you'll crave high-fat foods. So, when you're eating healthfully, it's easier to resist less nutritious foods.**

A vitamin pill cannot replace the natural nutrients in food. Some vitamins and minerals are actually not absorbed well unless they are provided in their natural form in the food itself. Also, the interaction of natural food chemicals provides numerous health benefits. By eating a good balance of foods, you won't need to worry about nutritional imbalances, because nutrients come in the right amounts and right proportions.

Nutritional wellness is a personal choice. It requires getting to know a little about nutrition and following through with wise food choices. The reward is a decrease in your odds of developing certain types of cancer, anemia, or heart disease.

# Index

# Index

# Guide to Citrus Juice Terms

**Florida Orange and Grapefruit Juices are available in a wide variety of choices. Use this guide to select the juice that suits your family's needs and tastes. There is no significant difference in nutrient content, regardless of the form.**

| Term | What It Means to You |
| --- | --- |
| FLORIDA SUNSHINE TREE | The products that carry this trademark on their label are produced from oranges or grapefruit grown only within the state of Florida. This trademark also guarantees that the juice is 100% pure and meets Florida's high-quality standards. |
| 100% PURE or 100% JUICE | These words on the front label guarantee that you are getting only juice, not a diluted juice beverage with sweeteners and water added. |
| FRESH-SQUEEZED JUICE | This juice is squeezed from fresh oranges or grapefruit and packaged in paperboard cartons, glass, or plastic containers; it is not pasteurized. |
| CHILLED, READY-TO-SERVE JUICE | This popular juice is usually found in the dairy section. |
| Not from Concentrate | This juice is pasteurized immediately after being squeezed. It has never been concentrated. |
| From Concentrate | This juice is manufactured as frozen concentrate, then reconstituted and pasteurized prior to packaging. |
| FROZEN CONCENTRATED JUICE | This product is made by removing water from juice and freezing the remaining liquid. It is reconstituted by adding water. |
| FRESH-FROZEN JUICE | This juice is squeezed and packaged or frozen without pasteurizing or further processing, and is usually found in frozen-food sections of the store. It is ready to drink after being thawed. |
| JUICE IN ASEPTIC CONTAINERS | This pasteurized juice or juice from concentrate is packaged in sterilized paperboard containers. It does not require refrigeration or freezing and is usually found on the shelf with other canned and bottled juices. |
| CANNED JUICE | This juice is pasteurized and sealed in cans to provide a shelf life of more than a year. Once opened, it should be refrigerated in a covered nonmetallic container and used within a week. |

# Fit, Fresh & Fast
## FLAVORS FROM FLORIDA

**For Meredith Publishing Services:**

Project Editor: **Sandra Mosley**

Project Designer: **Steve Lueder**

Contributing Project Editor: **Joyce Trollope**

Test Kitchen Director: **Sharon Stilwell**

Marketing Manager: **Sharon Vickery**

Editor-In-Chief: **Don Johnson**

Senior Project Editor: **James D. Blume**

Design Director: **Jann Williams**

Vice President, Publishing Director: **John Loughlin**

Publisher: **Mike Peterson**

Production Manager: **Ivan McDonald**

**For The Florida Department of Citrus:**

Executive Director: **Daniel L. Santangelo**

Processed Products Business Unit Director: **Eugene L. Richmond, Jr.**

Public Relations Director: **Ivy M. Leventhal**

Florida Citrus Commission: **Howard E. Sorrells, Chairman; George H. Austin; Martha R. Burke; Joe L. Davis, Sr.; Ronald P. Grigsby; James E. Huff; Rex V. McPherson, II; John L. Minton; William E. Owens; Margaret W. Paul; Talmadge G. Rice; and J. Brantley Schirard.**